SITES

&

Stories

Sara Goodwins

Loaghtan Books
Caardee
Dreemskerry Hill
Maughold
Isle of Man
IM7 1BE

Typesetting and origination by:
Loaghtan Books

Printed and bound by:
Lavenham Press Ltd

Published by Loaghtan Books

Website: www.loaghtanbooks.com

First published: March 2014

ISBN: 978 1 908060 08 2

Copyright © Sara Goodwins, 2014

Photographic copyright © George Hobbs, 2014
(unless otherwise indicated)

For Frances Chambers,
historian, writer, linguist,
proud Yorkshirewoman
and good friend

Front cover: Cregneash looking towards the Calf of Man

Rear cover: The Grand Union Camera Obscura on Douglas Head looking towards Douglas town and harbour

Title page: Castle Rushen with the harbour and mouth of the Silverburn in the foreground

CONTENTS

1   **Tynwald Hill**
The biggest hill on Mann   5
Climbing the legal mountain   9

2   **The Braaid**
Abode of mist   13
The plains of heaven   19

3   **The Douglas Corporation Horse Tramway**
Tracking round the bay   23
Horses still pulling their weight   27

4   **The Great Union Camera Obscura**
Less obscure   31
Elegantly old fashioned   35

5   **Peel Castle**
Merry wanderer of the night   39
Two saints and a castle   43

6   **Curragh Wildlife Park**
The lady in the lake   47
Around the world in eighty minutes   52

7   **Laxey**
Time enough   56
Fishing, mining and the gateway to Snaefell   63

8   **Castle Rushen**
Lights! Camera! ...   67
Mediaeval Magnificence   71

9   **The Grove**
Our feet may leave, but not our hearts   75
Taking you back in time   79

10   **Milner Tower**
Fifty-four degrees north, five degrees west   83
Demanding darkness   87

11   **Cregneash**
One dog and her man   91
Crofting life   95

12   **Snaefell**
Old man   99
Highpoint on Mann   102

Bibliography   106
Acknowledgements   107
Index   108

SITES MENTIONED IN THE TEXT

The sketch map below is intended only to give a rough idea of the location of the places mentioned in the text. Those travelling by car would be advised to use the 1:50,000 Ordnance Survey (OS) Landranger Map, sheet 95 (the pink one). Walkers should use either the OS map or the 1:25,000 Public Rights of Way and Outdoor Leisure Map published by the Isle of Man Government.

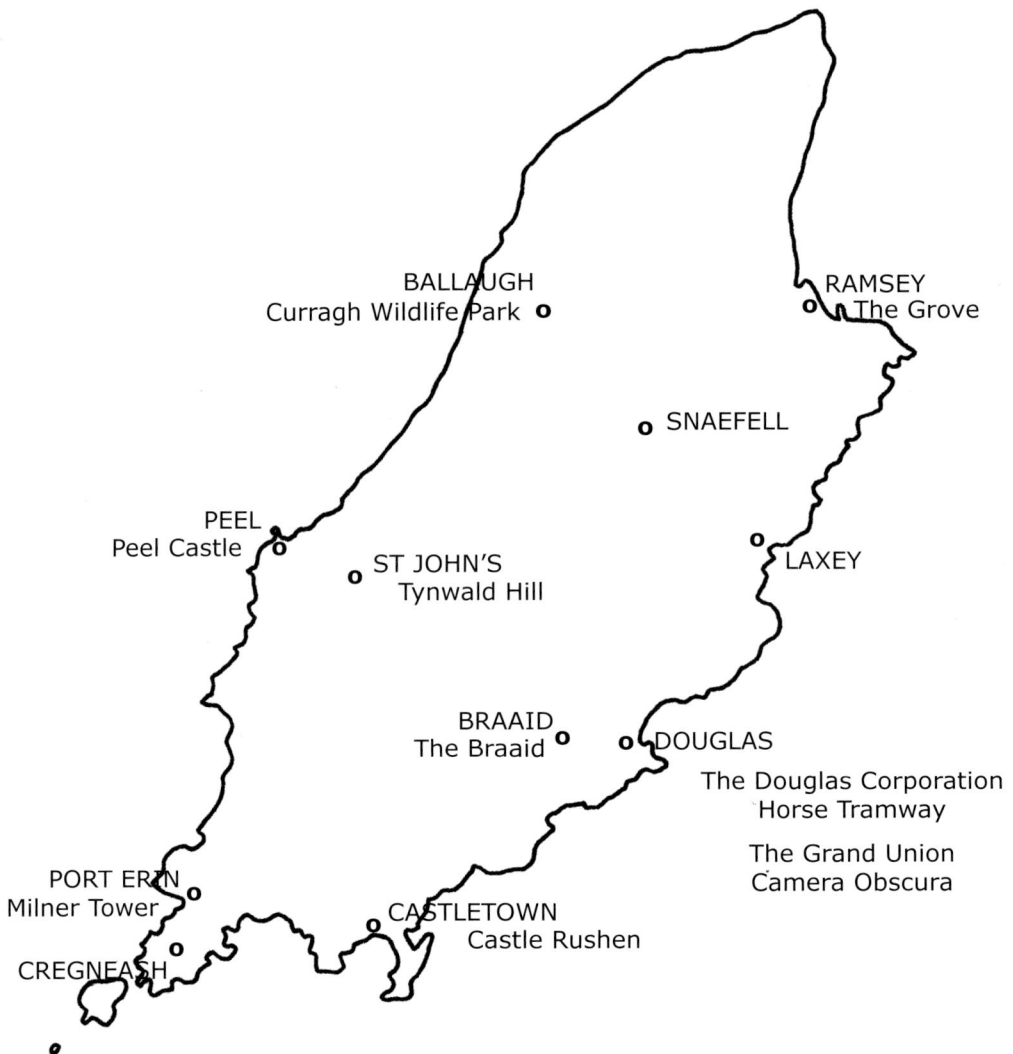

BALLAUGH
Curragh Wildlife Park

RAMSEY
The Grove

SNAEFELL

PEEL
Peel Castle

ST JOHN'S
Tynwald Hill

LAXEY

BRAAID
The Braaid

DOUGLAS

The Douglas Corporation
Horse Tramway

The Grand Union
Camera Obscura

PORT ERIN
Milner Tower

CASTLETOWN
Castle Rushen

CREGNEASH

THE BIGGEST HILL ON MANN

W hat are you *doing*?' Moirrey's whisper was more of a breathless squeak.
'Digging up a bit of the grass.'

'You can't do that! This is Tynwald Hill!'

'I'll put it back. No-one will notice.'

'And that makes it OK, does it? You vandalising the island's most historic site? The place where our forefathers met to read out their laws? The place where for centuries…'

'Oh shut up.' Startled Moirrey did. Stephen went on 'you sound just like old Mrs Corkhill at school. All this going on and on about the island's history and importance. It's crap. We're just a tiddly little island, surround by other islands not much bigger. That's why I'm off. America for me.'

' "The land of the free and home of the brave" ?' Her voice was sarcastic. He could even hear the quotation marks. Moirrey wanted to be an actress so milked anything with drama in it. You could even hear her punctuation.

'Yeah, if you like.'

'But what are you going to *do* there?'

'Dunno, but it's got to be better than working the boats or stacking tins in the Co-op, hasn't it?'

'You've got more choice than that.'

'Not with my qualifications – or lack of them.'

'That's your fault. You should have worked harder. Or at all.' The superiority in her voice was back. Stephen snapped at her:

'OK, if you don't want to help, bugger off. Don't know why you're here anyway.'

'Fine.' Moirrey hurled the torch at him – it bounced off the grass, so didn't break – and stomped off into the night. Scowling, Stephen carried on with his task.

The pageantry was over. The good and the great – and the humble – had gathered for the annual ritual at Tynwald Hill. The Sword of State had been paraded, the laws promulgated in Manx and English, the petitions accepted. Crowds had watched and

Tynwald Hill

THE TYNWALD CEREMONY, ISLE OF MAN

ISLE OF MAN £1
BDT
2006
The Agency Design

cameras had clicked. The visitor from Canada smiled slightly. The second Deemster had his sympathy. Difficult enough to struggle with a language which was obviously not your own, and to have to do so publically… He'd had the same trouble in Canada with French. Everyone had to speak it, at least up to a point, as all official paperwork had to be in both languages. He still worried about fielding questions from the Press when they were asked in French.

Hands in pockets he strolled over to the hill. On most other days people were allowed to walk on it freely, but not today. Today much of the surrounding area was roped off. He hadn't bargained for that. The flags were flying bravely and they'd had gorgeous weather. People were reluctant to leave.

A dark-haired woman gripping a clipboard and sheaf of notes walked briskly towards him. Or tried to. Her three-inch heels sank into the turf and she floundered. He watched her, amused, expecting her to pretend that there was nothing amiss. He was wrong. Almost without breaking step she slipped off her shoes, bent to pick them up, and continued towards him on bare feet. His eyebrows rose. He didn't think a clerk to the Canadian House of Commons would have been seen shoeless at the State Opening of Parliament… Then again, maybe they would. They were a pragmatic lot. He smiled a greeting as she approached:

'Ma'am.'

'You're American?'

'From Canada. How can I help you ma'am? You look like a stock dog sent to round up strays.' It was her turn to look surprised.

'I've never been called a dog before.' Then she realised what she'd said and blushed. The man's jaw dropped:

'Moirrey?' She looked up at him sharply, professional reserve to the fore.

'Do I know you?'

'We-ell, no, not now. But you did. I'm Steve. Steve Collister.'

For a moment she looked blank – that wasn't flattering he thought – then realisation dawned. 'Steen?' He smiled:

'I haven't heard the Manx version of my name for, oh, must be over twenty years.'

Sites and Stories

'What on earth are you doing here?'

'I've come home,' he said matter of factly.

'To a tiddly little island, surrounded by others not much bigger?' she said tartly. He threw back his head and laughed. 'You remembered!'

'How could I forget. I never saw you again.'

'Yes, I caught the boat didn't I? It was Canada and not the States in the end, but still a new start.' He was sober, 'did you mind?'

'I got over it.'

'Don't you want to know what I've been doing?'

'Making money,' she said flatly, 'I do read the papers, Steen. Or should I call you Mr Collister now?

'Don't be soft. I did OK.'

'More than OK. Don't you own one of the largest timber exporting firms in Canada?'

'Three Legs Forest Products, yeah.'

'Three Legs?' She raised an eyebrow.

'Sure.' He counted off on his fingers: 'Logging and harvesting. Solid wood products. Pulp and paper.'

'So nothing to do with the three legs of Mann?'

'I never had time for all that history stuff.'

'No, you didn't.' She sounded sad. He started to stroll round the Hill, taking her with him.

'What about you? Make it as an actress?' She snorted, 'likely isn't it?'

'Oh, I don't know. Plenty of people do.'

'And plenty more starve. I got a job working for the Court of Tynwald.

'So all this', he gestured at the panoply, 'is your work?'

'A small part of it perhaps. So… what brings you here?'

He looked at her. He had been going to make some excuse. Tell her that he'd been in

London and had thought he'd deke over to take in the old country. A few days' vacation perhaps, all that. He found he couldn't. They'd been good friends long ago. Given time it might have developed into something more. She deserved the truth.

'Pilgrimage,' he said shortly. She turned to him in surprise. Something in his face stopped her speaking.

'Remember last time we were here?' he said.

'Of course I do,' she was nettled, still uncomfortable with the memories.

'Remember old Mrs Corkhill?' She looked at him, puzzled now.

'Our old history teacher,' he prompted.

'Yes, I know,' she was irritated. 'I thought you didn't have time for "all that history stuff".' She was still doing it he noticed. Still talking in quotes.

'Maybe I had more time for it than either of us knew. Remember what she said?'

'About the history of Tynwald Hill?'

'No. About how it was made.' She shook her head, not because she didn't remember, but because she didn't understand.

'She said that every parish in the island had contributed earth to the building of the hill. Consequently when you were standing on Tynwald Hill you were touching the whole of the Isle of Man.'

He reached into his pockets and pulled out a small and scruffy plastic bag. He held it up for her to see. It contained about a tablespoon full of earth.

'When I left, I took a bit of the Hill with me. For luck.' She stared, her eyes filling with tears. Hospice Isle of Man had been approached about the right way for someone to make a huge donation. An anonymous donation. The Department of Health was involved in negotiations. Despite the island's extremely efficient grapevine no word of it had yet leaked out.

'I've come to put something back,' he said simply.

TYNWALD HILL (WHERE MANX LAWS ARE MADE)

84234. JV.

CLIMBING THE LEGAL MOUNTAIN

Tynwald Hill is a strange mix of the very impressive and rather underwhelming. It is possible to pass it on the A1 without noticing it – OK you'd have to be fairly unobservant – but the hill has no great stature or silhouette to make is stand out and in fact sits quite modestly within its grassy field. Other historic sites on Mann are more instantly impressive, but no other site in the world links the present with the past in the same way as Tynwald Hill.

The Isle of Man is rightly proud of its Viking heritage and most of the political and legal structure of the island can be traced directly to the organisation of the Norsemen. Communities in Scandinavia lived in small tribal groups isolated by forest and fjord. To ensure that tribal harmony was maintained and larger issues discussed, the free men of the community met periodically to debate, affirm, amend or add to existing tribal laws.

In Norse the meeting was known as a *thing*. Several communities coming together for a joint meeting on larger issues constituted an *all-thing*. The ancient tradition is echoed today in the names of the parliaments of various Scandinavian countries. Even Shetland and Orkney had their parliaments, both at places called Tingwall. Only in the Isle of Man is the tradition unbroken in the oldest continuous parliament in the world – Tynwald.

The assembly field where a *thing* took place was called the *thing-völlr*, which is where Tynwald gets its name. The leaders of the assembly met on a low hill which was linked by a processional way stretching eastwards to a place of worship which was also used as a place of judgement or courthouse. If people are going to travel some distance for an official meeting, their supporters will need entertaining while they do so. The official meeting site was surrounded by banks to mark physically the philosophical separation between the official discussions and ceremonies happening inside, and the celebrations and junketings of a less ambassadorial nature which were happening outside. The layout of Tynwald Hill and the processional way to the church was constructed as it is now during the nineteenth century – St John's Church was consecrated in 1849 replacing a much older series of religious buildings – but reproduces almost exactly the layout of the early *things*.

The Royal Chapel in St John's has an essential role in Tynwald Day and, as such, is unique for two reasons. Not only is it the only Christian church where a government transacts business (albeit only once a year during the Tynwald ceremonies), but is also the only Christian church with an area which is not consecrated. The named seats where members of the House of Keys sit, although inside the religious building is spiritually not part of it. By this means any of the Keys who are non-Christian can be accommodated.

The Hill of St John's Church, or *Cronk Keeill Eoin*, is the name by which Tynwald Hill is known in Manx. The mound has a diameter of seventy six feet at the base, and faces onto a processional way which is 360 feet long. It is twelve feet tall stepped into four stages or circular platforms, each about three feet higher than the one below. On Tynwald Day each of the tiers represent part of the hierarchy in the Court of Tynwald, and its members are seated accordingly.

Seated on the top tier of Tynwald Hill therefore is the Lord of Man and their consort, currently Queen Elizabeth II, or the Lord's representative the Lieutenant Governor. The President of Tynwald, the Lord Bishop of Sodor & Man, the Surgeon to the Household, the Sword Bearer and the Members and Clerk

St John's church, interior (above and right). The squarish arrangement of seats just before the chancel is where the Keys sit to transact government business. Each seat is named. The speaker's seat is marked by a crest, centre right in the upper picture

5 July 2013. The Deemsters promulgate the laws in Manx and English during the ancient ceremony held each year on Tynwald Hill. Photograph courtesy of the Court of Tynwald

of the Legislative Council, are also seated on the top tier so it can get a bit crowded.

The Manx parliament is divided into two chambers, the House of Keys and the Legislative Council. The two chambers are roughly equivalent to the Houses of Commons and Lords in the Westminster parliament, although they do not have precisely the same executive function. Apart from the President of Tynwald, the Lord Bishop of Sodor & Man and the Attorney General who are Members of the Legislative Council by right, eight further members are elected to the upper house, by the Keys.

The lower chamber of the Manx parliament, the House of Keys, has twenty four members. Indeed its Manx name, *Yn Chiare as Feed*, means 'the Twenty Four'. On Tynwald Day the second tier down is therefore occupied by the House of Keys, its secretary and chaplain.

On the third tier sit the High Bailiff, the representative of the Commission of the Peace, the Chief Registrar, the Mayor of Douglas, the Chairmen of Commissioners from Castletown, Peel, Ramsey, Laxey, Onchan, Port Erin and Port St Mary, the Archdeacon, the Vicar General, the clergy of various denominations and the Chief Constable.

Seated on the fourth and lowest tier are the four Coroners, *Yn Lhaihder* (The Reader), and the captains of the seventeen parishes. The fourth tier also carries the two lecterns used by the two Deemsters or judges when they proclaim the laws enacted during the previous year. The First Deemster stands at the lectern on the south side of the hill to promulgate the new laws in English, followed by the Second Deemster who stands at the lectern on the north side to promulgate them in Manx. Tynwald Hill and most of St John's is in the parish of German so the annual ritual gives rise to the local pun of Manx laws having to be read in English, in Manx and in German.

No record exists stating when Tynwald first began, although as an established part of Norse culture, it's likely that local *things*, rather like a meeting of a local council, would have been introduced almost as soon as the Norsemen began establishing settlements. The island celebrated 1,000 years of Tynwald in 1979, which suggests that the national *thing* was established, or at least formalised by 979 when the island owed allegiance to Earl Haakan Sigurdsson, King of Norway. Midsummer was a time when isolated communities got together to celebrate, and it would have saved much travelling if the *thing* took place at the same time. The Court of Tynwald still meets on Tynwald Hill, on 5 July, Old Midsummer's Day.

The ancient traditions of Tynwald Day have changed very little over centuries. One of the earliest records of the day's ceremonies dates from 1422. Sir John Stanley, King of Mann, was advised 'Upon the Hill of Tynwald sitt in a chaire covered with a royall cloath and cushions, and your visage unto the east, your swoard before you, houlden with the pointe upwards...' Six hundred years later the seating is still as stated and the Manx Sword of State is still carried upright in front of the Lord of Man or their representative the Lieutenant Governor. The sword is thought to date from the early fifteenth century – the blade was replaced probably in the late fifteenth or early sixteenth century – and may have been the Sword borne before Sir John Stanley at the 1422 Tynwald.

St John's church plays a large role in the Tynwald ceremonies but other traditions hark back to religions which existed on Mann before the church of Christ. The Irish sea god Manannan is often credited as being the protector of the Isle of Mann, and the processional way from the hill to the church is strewn with marram grass in tribute to him. A ballad dating from the eighteenth century suggests that marram was cut from the coastal dunes where it grows naturally, and was carried to the top of South Barrule where it was left to pay rent to Manannan. The local name for marram grass in English is 'bent', although it's *shaslagh* in Manx.

Those taking part in Tynwald Day are protected from head to toe. As well as walking over marram grass they also wear a sprig of mugwort or *Bollan-feaill-Eoin* (literally the wort of the vigil of John). Traditionally worn in the hat or on the head, mugwort protects against supernatural harm. Despite the similarity of names, the plant is not the same as St John's Wort which does not grow naturally on Mann. Sometimes called bollan bane, wearers of mugwort are, by Scandinavian custom, also demonstrating loyalty to their monarch.

Although Tynwald has met in traditional vein for over a thousand years, it has not always met at St John's. Sites of other Tynwalds certainly existed – the 1422 Tynwald mentioned above met at Kirk Michael – and two other 'tynwald hills' are thought to have been identified. One is near West Baldwin Reservoir north of St Luke's church, while the other is at Cronk Urley upstream from Glen Wyllin. No-one knows when the Tynwald Hill at St John's was originally built, although there are suggestions that it may originally have been the burial site of a Bronze Age chieftain, as such barrows occasionally formed local assembly places.

Traditionally *thing* sites included a handful of earth brought from each tribal territory, so that all tribal representatives could think of themselves as being on their homeground and, perhaps more importantly, be governed by the laws of hospitality. Such laws would prevent violence from breaking out between volatile tribal leaders. Even today one of the coroners and *Yn Lhaihder* 'fences' the court, the coroner in English and *Yn Lhaihder* in Manx. Fencing is a proclamation to all those present that no disturbance will be tolerated and that everyone should answer to their names when called. No weapons, apart from the Sword of State, are permitted within the symbolic fence.

In keeping with tradition Tynwald Hill is said to contain earth drawn from all seventeen parishes in the island. While the Keys and Legislative Council are unlikely to liven up Tynwald Day by indulging in a bout of fisticuffs, it's a lovely idea that not only the people but also the land on which they live are all represented on the ancient hill in St John's.

ABODE OF MIST

Asmund slammed the door of his car and went round to the boot. As always he noted with pride his personalised number plate, A 5 MAN. As a child he'd hated his name, labelled with something odd and teased about it. Now he loved it, although he was careful not to say so. No-one else in the re-enactment group had a name which was both Manx and Viking.

Glancing casually at the swirling mist he spared a thought for what odd weather they were having. The fog had come down so fast! He opened the boot and carefully lifted out his sword. He was very proud of that sword. He'd made it himself at one of those have-a-go blacksmithing events. He'd done the lot: forming, grinding, sharpening – he'd particularly enjoyed the sharpening – and decoration. The geometric decoration he'd intended to add to the pommel had gone wrong and he'd had to be content with just a moulded knob, but the shaping of the guard had worked. The leather-wrapped wooden grip, and leather-covered

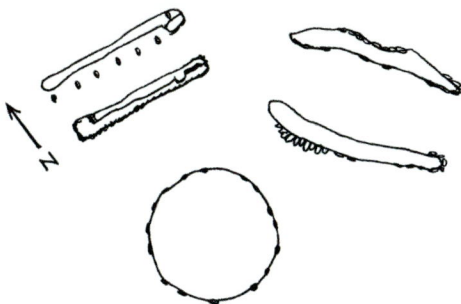

A plan of The Braaid showing the outline of two longhouses and a roundhouse. The orientation is the same as for the photograph

wooden sheath had been made by another member of the group. Asmund dismissed them; he was only interested in the blade. He'd even named it. *Gunnlogi*, Battle-blaze. One day he was going to learn how to fight with it.

He imagined wielding it, striking sparks from the blade, and the fear on his opponents' faces. That'd show them. He was a bit hazy about who 'they' were, but certainly the outdoor types who sneered. As if he didn't know. In fact they meant him to know. Meant him to be sure that he was only allowed to tag along because he did the group's books and kept them solvent.

These two images are viewed from almost the same place. The sketch of how The Braaid might have looked is taken from one of the site's information boards

He glanced, dissatisfied, at the car. It was new and he'd parked it as far into the gateway as he could, but it was still on the road. This fog! He knew there was a lay by somewhere off the A24, but he hadn't found it. Presumably everyone else had arrived and parked before the fog came down. He felt a bit light headed; it must have been all the beer he'd drank yesterday. He wasn't really used to it. Had he really boasted that he could fight as well as any Viking now he had a proper sword? (*Groan!*) And he was very late. It was being stopped by those traffic cops which had been the problem. They'd thought it very funny to breathalyse a driver dressed in full Viking kit. He wondered whether they'd have been so happy if they'd known he had *Gunnlogi* in the boot. He had a momentary picture of him drawing it and defying them replaced immediately by another of him in clink. Slinging the baldric onto his shoulder he opened the gate and stumbled down the rough grass.

He couldn't hear the re-enactment group, but sounds were muffled in the fog and most of the setting up must have been done by now. In fact he could smell dinner cooking, something roasting and delicious. A couple of Viking long houses loomed out of the mist. Bill and his mates had done a fantastic job, they looked really authentic. Last night in the pub they'd boasted about how they'd made the long houses out of original materials, but prefabricated; they could be brought to any site on a lorry, temporarily erected and still look the part. Manx National Heritage had allowed the Manx-Norsk Viking re-enactment group to use one of the original Viking sites on the island but had baulked at permitting temporary buildings to be erected on the remains of the original Viking longhouses. Consequently the prefabricated wooden walls were going to have to rest unauthentically on the grass. The Manx contingent and their Norwegian guests were to live as Vikings for three days. The bank holiday weekend was a celebration of the island's Viking heritage, and the MaNorVik camp at the Braaid was one of the highlights. Pity about the rubbish weather; they wouldn't get many visitors today.

A woman came out of the nearest longhouse. Asmund didn't know her, but she was obviously a member of the team. Her costume was perfect, long linen shift covered by shorter woollen dress was held up with metal brooches and belted with a colourful braid. A row of beads hung between the brooches and she had long fair hair. Asmund approached her tentatively:

'Sorry. I'm a bit late. Know where Pete is? I'm not sure what he wants me to do.' The woman's welcoming smile froze. Straightening she assessed Asmund warily and then turned and went back into the longhouse. He shrugged. Presumably she was one of the Norwegian group. As he wandered further into the camp she came back with another man, a big man, also in costume. She gestured towards the newcomer. Asmund pinned his smile back onto his face and asked his question again. The man did not reply. Something about his silence was worrying. Raising a hand Asmund wandered past the first longhouse towards the second. Presumably the Manx contingent were in there.

Glancing back Asmund realised that the big man had been joined by another. Both were watching him,

Above and left: clothing typical of that worn by men and women throughout the Norse regions modelled by a member of Hurstwic. Women were highly respected in Viking society and although they took no part in raids, did participate in journeys of exploration and settlement. The group's main focus is to research and practice Viking-age fighting moves as explained in the Sagas of Iceland and elsewhere. Photographs © hurstwic.org

15

discussing his appearance in low voices. He didn't understand the guttural language and he didn't feel comfortable with their pointing and jabbering. He'd seen enough pub fights to recognise the beginnings of trouble. He speeded up but was also confused. Why should they be so alarmed? He wasn't looking for trouble, he never did (except in his imagination) and surely neither were they. He glanced back nervously. The two men had become five, the original woman joined by two others. All were watching him.

He reached the Manx longhouse and was just about to go in when his eye was caught by the base of one of the plank walls. It rested on stone footings. Not only that but grass and weeds had grown into the rock and were beginning to twine up the wooden walls. Now Bill was a good craftsman. A very good craftsman. But not even Bill could make a prefabricated Viking longhouse look as though it was rooted to the site. And Manx National Heritage would certainly not allow MaNorVik to go digging into one of their national monuments.

Then Asmund saw the child. She was blonde, barefooted and probably no more than six or seven. The simple drop spindle she carried twirled between her fingers, spinning wool into yarn with speed and precision. No modern child could do that. Certainly not one that young. What was… happening…?

No, he was being daft. This was some sort of trick. Yes; that was it. Another of the small cruelties stretching back to childhood. Always an outsider; never accepted.

Asmund, his back to the longhouse wall, looked round, expecting to see Pete and his mates hiding somewhere, sniggering. The mist still swirled but had lifted slightly. A rough pen containing half a dozen small cows was in one corner. Children tugged at a goat on a string. A wild-eyed cat slunk under one of the longhouses. Hay was stacked against a wooden wall. Further away, boys in leggings practised archery and swordsmanship under the tuition of a long-legged man with a scar across his face. Women gossiped over their *nålebinding*. One worked at a tablet loom, another taught her daughter finger braiding. To one side a woman with cropped hair and wearing a thrall collar was grinding corn on a hand quern.

Everything looked… real. No, no, it was impossible. How could these people be real? Wildly he looked from side to side. He must be dreaming. He must be dreaming. Perhaps Pete had slipped a mickey fin into his beer last night and he was still asleep.

He didn't feel asleep. He felt cold. And damp. And… frightened. What was *happening?*

Other men had appeared, some with dogs. The big man, presumably the leader, had taken one step towards him. Then… Asmund's phone rang. A tune from the Jorvik panpipe drifted out across the tension. For a moment he couldn't believe what he was hearing.

The reaction was startling. The entire community broke into agitated whispering, children backed away, women scooped babies into their arms, and even one or two of the men took a pace backwards. Fear was written on their faces. *Seiðr!* Witchcraft!

Asmund grabbed his chance. He ran.

The crowd broke into howls and gave chase. His buttoned leather shoes slipped on the grass. He wasn't used to running. He was an *accountant* for goodness sake! *Gunnlogi* banged against his back. His sword! For a moment he contemplated using it. He saw himself drawing the bright blade. As he had so often before he imagined wielding it against massed foes and them falling back. For a brief moment his fantasy warmed him. Cold realisation soon doused such thoughts. It was the sword which had made him such a laughing stock. The rest of the group knew he was pretending. Fantasising. Knew he couldn't use it.

If these really were… somehow… Vikings (*surely not!*), then they knew a damn sight more about fighting than he ever would. This must be a trick. It must! It was that boast of his… Someone had set him up…

A roar behind him forced him onwards. The rational part of his mind told him not to be silly. His instinct for preservation kept his legs moving. The mist swirled, disorientating him. He didn't know where he was. He tried to find a fence. He was heading for his car – if his car was still there – and expected to follow a fence. But there was no fence. After several hundred yards it seemed that there was no road and no car either. Sobbing he forced himself on. Perhaps a house? Or… where was the nearest farm… ?

They were gaining. Of course they were. They were hunters, fit,

Viking chess player, outside the post office, Parliament Street, Ramsey

depending on their skills to stay alive. They were almost on him. Perhaps he could hide in the mist? (*From dogs?*)

His mobile rang again, giving him away.

Spinning he fumbled with the scabbard, tugging the sword free. It was better than nothing. And it was a good sword. Clumsily he swung it. There was nothing there. No running men. No dogs.

His phone called again. The panpipe. He'd have to change the ring tone. A nice bell perhaps. He fumbled in the leather pouch at his belt. Cold sweat ran down his face. Could he call for help? But what would he *say*? Shaking, he pressed the call receive button

'Asmund? Where are you mate?' Pete, the re-enactment organiser sounded only mildly interested. 'Well, never mind.' One of the others said something Asmund didn't catch. He caught the scorn in the group's laughter though. 'Look, mate, the fog made it impossible. We called it off for today. Try to set up tomorrow. We're in that pub we went to last night, the one in Peel…' Asmund's hand dropped. His phone dropped from his fingers. He gripped the sword he had made. The sword he didn't know how to use. Shadows were gathering. Men with rough cloaks and leather skullcaps, appeared through the fog. Thick set dogs with teeth bared slunk at their heels. The pack circled, swords held negligently, competently. At his feet the mobile chattered insistently:

'Asmund.'

'Asmund?'

'*Asmund!*'

THE PLAINS OF HEAVEN

Mist was important in Norse mythology. Nilfheim was the dwelling place of mist and the first of the nine worlds. The origin of all living things was Hvelgelmir, the oldest of the three wells, and it existed in the mists of Nilfheim. Vikings were fairly relaxed about their religion, but they took their story-telling seriously. For Vikings, mythology and religion blended with oral history to provide a background against which they judged themselves and their world.

Very little is known about the practice of Viking religion, except that the tribal leader acted as some sort of priest. Magic, on the other hand, is fairly well documented, and usually although not exclusively performed by women. Some of the celebrations of Viking faith may also be performed by women. *Seiðr* is the most common form of magic, often translated as witchcraft, but covers 'good' magic as well as that intended to harm. The most characteristic element of *seiðr*, however, seems to have been magic which affects the mind, prompting the recipient to suffer from forgetfulness, illusions or madness.

Today the warlike invaders from the north are known as Vikings, but they may not have called themselves that, or if they did they weren't using the word to describe their race, clan or tribe, but rather their activity. In Old Norse a *vik* is a creek, bay or river estuary and therefore a good place to attack. The word *viking* can be used as a noun meaning a raid from the sea, or as a verb such as 'going viking', while a *vikingr* is a sea warrior. Vikings were therefore seafaring raiders, but very few of them were what could be called professionals, i.e. full-time warriors. Most were farmers looking to eke out their living. They might, for example, become a *vikingr* for a season or two before settling down, or return to raiding after a bad harvest. Only a few of the Norsemen were Vikings at any one time but most were or had been Vikings some of the time. Eventually the rich land probably prompted those without farms and families of their own to stay and settle.

ISLE OF MAN — THAMES DIAMOND JUBILEE PAGEANT

50P

EJC DESIGN 2012 BDT

The Braaid is the only site on the Isle of Man which appears to show a continuity between the Celtic inhabitants and the Viking invaders. Celtic dwellings are round, Viking dwellings rectangular and both appear at The Braaid. It is in fact a farmstead in an area sometimes known as The Plains of Heaven. As both

styles of architecture appear so close together, and as the Celtic roundhouse continued in use after the longhouses were built it looks as though the takeover was relatively uncontested. Some of the Viking invaders brought their wives with them but many married native Celtic women, possibly the daughters of the families they conquered, and that may have been what happened here.

Apart from the shape, the construction of the two types of dwelling also differed, although both were designed to house all the people working on the farm. Celtic roundhouses were built by digging a circular gulley into which the timbers supporting the wall were embedded. The walls were woven, huge oak rafters rested on the load-bearing was thatched and, finally, the walls daubed with

The Viking Boats at Peel, Isle of Man

and timbers. The roof a mixture of clay and dung to make a kind of plaster. Viking longhouses tended to have stone-built footings, while the walls were made of wooden planks, logs, wattle and daub or turf. The pitched roofs were thatched or again could be turfed. Frequently, as at The Braaid, the walls of longhouses curved slightly outwards from either end, so that they were wider in the middle. The shape mimicked that of upturned longboats, with the ends missing, although whether that was deliberate, unconscious or accidental is open to question. Of course neither longhouses nor roundhouses were all built to exactly the same blueprint everywhere; people varied the construction according to what materials were available locally.

At The Braaid, the smaller of the longhouses was probably a cattle byre. Cattle were probably the most important domestic animal, indicated by the fact that a man's wealth was judged by the number of cows he owned or could buy. Sheep were also common and important as providers of wool, meat and milk. The Gutefår is the oldest breed of sheep found in Scandinavia and is thought to be the breed which the Norsemen would have known and farmed. Vikings are credited with introducing the Manx Loaghtan sheep to the island, and the two breeds, Gutefår and Loaghtan, are remarkably similar. Loaghtan sheep are small, hardy, lack wool on their face and legs and have four and occasionally six horns. They also shed their wool naturally, so do not need to be shorn; Norse women would have gathered the wool from hedges and fields.

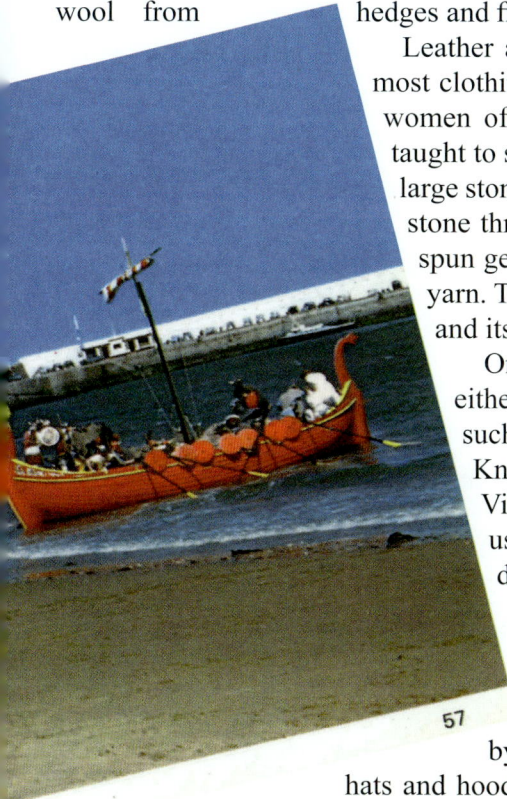

Leather and hide were very important for battle clothing, but most clothing for domestic use was made of wool or linen by the women of the household. Girls from a very young age were taught to spin using a simple drop spindle consisting mainly of a large stone with a hole in it. Small strands of wool are tied to the stone through the hole, the stone is suspended from the wool, spun gently and, by revolving, forms the strands of wool into yarn. The weight of the stone keeps the yarn straight and taut, and its rotation gives the yarn twist and therefore strength.

Once a sufficient amount of yarn was produced it was either woven on a frame loom, or turned into small garments such as socks or hats by a process called *nålebinding*. Knitting using two knitting pins was unknown among the Vikings; *nålebinding* produces a thick knitted-like fabric using a bone or wooden needle similar to a large flat darning needle.

Just like today, good clothing was a sign of the wearer's importance. For men, swords and iron helmets were a status symbol as both were costly to make. Close-fitting leather caps were probably worn by many of the rank and file in battle, although woollen hats and hoods would have been more usual in a domestic setting.

All free men were expected to own weapons, and tribal leaders were expected to provide them for their men. The Norse culture extolled the virtues of warfare and Viking men would have been prized by their community for their proficiency in arms and indifference to danger.

Cloaks were held in place by finely wrought pins, everyone who could afford it wore jewellery, and hair for both sexes was worn long and braided. Vikings were a very clean people, regularly washed and combed their hair – both sexes carried personal combs – washed their faces and hands daily, and usually bathed about once a week.

Slavery was common in Viking society, with slaves constituting much of their master's portable property. Slaves captured in raids were *anauð*, as opposed to *þræll* or thralls which were unfree servants of the Viking's own tribes. Slaves were identified by their short hair

57

ISLE of MAN

IOM

Manx National Heritage
Celtic Islanders and Viking Invaders
Manx National Heritage 2004 BDT
The Agency Ltd.

and thrall ring, which looked like a dog's collar made of iron riveted together and which was impossible to take off.

Instrumental music seems to have been a rare skill among the Vikings, possibly because time for practicing an instrument would have had to be borrowed from time spent training in skills at arms. Even so, some remains of several instruments dating from the Viking era have been found by archaeology, although none on Mann (yet!). One of the earliest instruments

to survive was found during an excavation at Coppergate in York, England and is of a tenth century pan pipe. When played, reproductions of the pipe sound a five-note scale from A to E. Other instruments familiar to Vikings include simple trumpets made out of wood or cow's horn, lyres or harps, and hand drums similar to the Irish bodhrán.

If players of instruments were not particularly regarded, bards and storytellers were highly prized in the Norse culture. Stories and sagas were often sung or intoned, so vocal music was common. Storytellers were highly respected, partly because they provided entertainment during the long winter darkness – the Viking equivalent of television – and partly because Viking history was passed down orally. Little if anything was written down until centuries later, so the bards became the record keepers for the community. Much of what we know about those living in farming communities such as The Braaid comes not from archaeology, but from the sagas and tales which still survive today:

'*Spyrja vitrir menn konung hvað gegnast muni í þessu máli er sjá maður segir.*' [The wisest of them asked what truth there might be in the story this man had told.] *Laxdaela Saga*, chapter 21.

TRACKING ROUND THE BAY

Roger shook his head when the little girl asked whether she could feed the horse. Looking nervously at her Mum she did so anyway. He smelled something minty before the illicit sweet disappeared off the flattened palm.

He sighed and, her bravery demonstrated, the little girl scuttled back to her Mum. Clive, the conductor, said something reassuring and patted the 'motive power unit, a.k.a. horse'. He always said that, and the joke was beginning to pall. He was a good conductor though, knowledgeable about the trams and horses, helping people with bags and directions, and always spotting passengers waiting by the side of the road. That saved Roger the bother of worrying about missing customers. He could concentrate on watching out for traffic and making sure that the tram got from one end of Douglas promenade to the other, safely and in good time. It was hot today and they'd probably be busy.

Standing by the tram at the sea terminal, waiting for the next lot of passengers, Roger reflected that horses have a relatively simple life. A few people were worried about cruelty, but the tram horses enjoyed their work. It was not difficult, although could be stressful at times if traffic was dense, but they saw lots to interest them and they didn't have to do too much. A couple of return trips of the promenade, about eight miles in total, and that was their shift for the day. After that they went back to the stables for rubbing down, feeding and then, like their human bosses, a gossip with their mates.

fresh one would be standing waiting with the stablehand. He didn't think it was this turn that they did the switch, but couldn't quite remember. No… no replacement waiting so no need to stop, and they trotted on to the Terminus Tavern. They'd get a bit of a break there and he could do with something to drink. He didn't eat while he was working – apart from the odd snack that was – but he couldn't go long without drinking something. Not in this heat. It was Clive's turn to get them in, he thought.

As often happened, passengers from the electric railway were waiting to board the horse tram. Most people stood back while the tram's three crew members – driver, conductor and horse – walked and clopped from one end of their vehicle to the other. A few, unused to the slower pace of life, got in the way and tried to board the tram too soon, as if they were worried it would leave without them. Roger didn't fuss. He knew his conductor would explain. He didn't have much of a sense of humour, but he did wonder, wryly, whether some people thought the tram would move on its own. A few minutes break, a quick drink, and they were off again. It was odd; the view of the line from this direction looked totally different. It all added interest to the job.

They worked steadily for another hour. Next time round, when they passed the tram stables heading north, Jenny and Ted were waiting for them so they stopped in the middle of the road to change horses. Visitors always liked to see the leisurely way the team strolled across, making all the modern traffic wait. Quite right too, thought Roger, as Jenny the stablehand accompanied Ted's unhurried progress across the road. We were here first. Jenny had a message for his driver, so Roger passed the time of day with Ted. An hour later, rubbed down and fed, he was dozing quietly in his stall with the rest of his herd.

HORSES STILL PULLING THEIR WEIGHT

Of the 140 horse tramways which once provided public transport in the British Isles, the Douglas Corporation horse tram is the only one still operating. Opened in 1876, the tramway still provides transport along Douglas promenade during the summer months as it has done for nearly 140 years.

The Douglas Bay Horse Tramway, as it is officially called, was once owned by the company which owned the Manx Electric Railway. When the MER went into liquidation at the beginning of the twentieth century, the horse trams were taken over by Douglas Corporation and have been operated by the corporation since 1902.

Tram horses used to be imported from Ireland, but are now bred for the purpose on the Isle of Man. From 1974 to 1999 Douglas Corporation bred its own horses, but now purchases them from the Ballafayle Stud in Maughold when they are yearlings. Training for the tram horses begins in the field and then moves to the beach at Douglas; they start work at age four. To ease them into the job, new horses take the quieter shifts with the more experienced drivers. Depending on health and need, horses usually work each summer season until they are about eighteen when they retire from regular duties and go to live in the Home of Rest for Old Horses on Richmond Hill near Douglas. During the winter they are put out to grass and take part in occasional ploughing matches or appear at agricultural shows. Sometimes people remark how alike many of the tram horses look. Of course they do; most of them are related! The horse trams are the equine equivalent of a family-run business.

At the time of writing sixteen horses are needed to operate the service, and the corporation owns a further eleven, which are mostly young horses and those in training. The major cost of running a horse-hauled tramway has always been the cost of the horses and their accommodation, food, shoes, stablehands' wages and vet's bills. The Douglas tramway is no exception. Horses are stabled at Summerhill during the summer months, the old stalls having been replaced by loose boxes during 2000 and 2004, as the trams now run less frequently and so need fewer horses. Unlike stalls where animals are tethered, loose boxes have doors which shut their occupants in and so allow the horses to move around freely. The horses can also see each other over the sides of their boxes; as herd animals they are reassured if they know that they're not on their own. Each horse has its own box, in which it lives for the duration of the summer season.

When they are working every horse does two round trips (four lengths) of Douglas promenade per day, which amounts to about eight miles. Hauling the tram the length of Douglas promenade takes around twenty minutes depending on traffic and the number of passengers wanting to get on and off, so a horse works a maximum of two hours each day. So much road work obviously wears shoes down quite quickly and each horse is reshod every four weeks, unless a shoe works loose in which case it is either refitted or the entire set replaced.

The harness consists of a bridle, usually with blinkers, collar with hames, which are metal rings, and traces which are the leather strap running from the hame to the tram, with which the horse pulls the tram along. Each horse has its own collar made especially to fit and with the horse's name on a plaque hanging beneath it. A horse working in another animal's tack would be like a person walking in someone else's shoes, at best impractical and uncomfortable, at worst causing sores which can prevent the animal working until it recovered. Comfortable harness is essential both for the health of the horse and the efficient running of the tramway; sick or injured horses still have to be fed and tended.

Compared with the typical trappings of a carriage horse, the harness is minimalist. A carriage designed for road work has shafts to keep the horse and carriage together as an integral unit, and so has more leatherwork to ensure that the horse is attached safely between the shafts and won't hurt itself, or part company with or damage its vehicle. Carriage harness also tends to be more highly decorated. On a tramway the rails stop the carriage yawing, so no shafts are needed, and, except on special occasions, decoration is usually viewed as something extra to keep clean. The horse therefore has unusual freedom of lateral movement. This can be an advantage if motor vehicles get a bit too close – the horse, if not the tram, can get out of the way.

Horses are taught to stay between the tram lines and to respond to voice commands, the sound of the brake being applied and the conductor's whistle. It is the driver and not the horse who stops the tram rolling, by applying the brakes. When the horse hears the brake applied

and feels the extra tension in the traces, it knows the vehicle will be slowing down and so stops pulling. The horse is trained to slow down and stop in time with the tram so that it doesn't waste energy pulling against the brake, and doesn't stop suddenly and have the vehicle run into its legs.

The most demanding part of the horse's job is to get the tram moving. Horses are trained to lean into the collar, using the powerful muscles in their back legs to ease the tram forward. Springs attached between the end of the trace and the tramcar also make starting easier. Once the tram is moving, keeping it so uses virtually the same amount of energy regardless of speed – within reason of course – so the horse is encouraged to move promptly from a walk to a trot. Perhaps contra intuitively, trotting makes the load on the horse easier, probably because the two-time gait consists entirely of forward motion. The rolling four-time gait of the walk includes moments when the horse's action works against the forward motion of the tram and so, momentarily, allows it to slow down. For a horse, when pulling something, walking is actually harder work than trotting.

Each tram horse weighs around a ton. With a freestanding four-wheeled road vehicle draft horses can pull about twice their own weight comfortably; two-wheeled vehicles

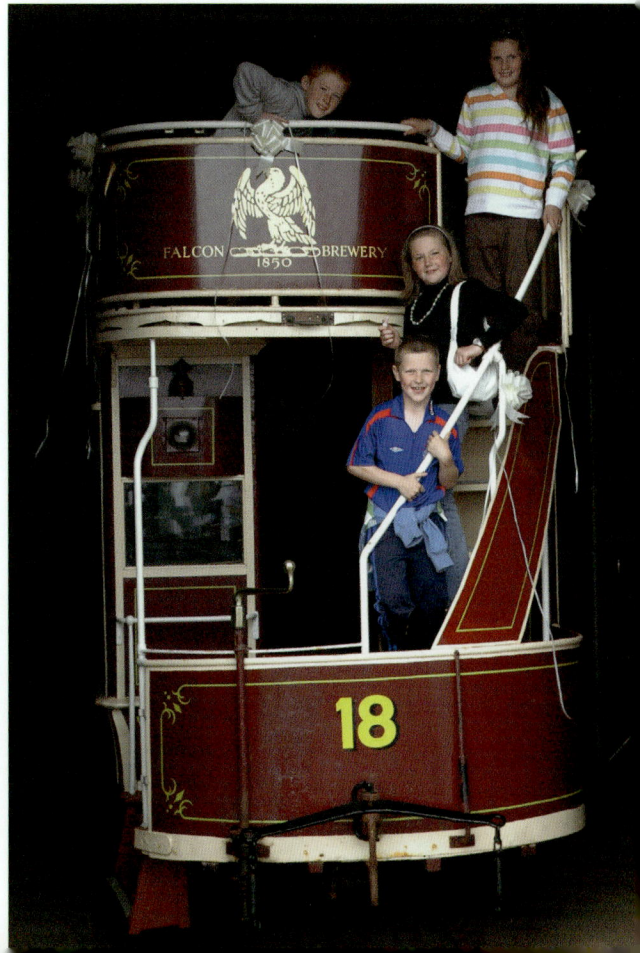

'lean' on the horse so it can pull less heavy loads in a two wheeler, as it has to carry weight as well as pull it. A vehicle running on rails, such as a tram, however, has less friction, so tram horses can comfortably haul about four times their own body weight.

The Douglas tramway has a number of single-deck vehicles of differing sizes and shapes. Cars which are totally enclosed, with roof and windows, tend to be smaller, while those which lack almost everything apart from seats tend to be longer, so an empty tramcar can generally be thought to weigh about two tons. People vary in weight of course, but traditionally the adage went: 'fifteen inches equals one bum; fifteen bums equal one ton'. As people have got bigger this 'rule of bum' no longer applies as fewer people fit on each car, but a full load of passengers will still double the tramcar's unladen weight. One horse is therefore asked to haul a maximum of around four tons, which is about right.

The horse tram fleet once included six double-decker trams purchased second hand from a defunct tramway in South Shields. The extra superstructure meant that the unladen weight of these was obviously higher than single-decked trams, and they also carried a larger number of passengers. Tramway historians are divided in their opinion about whether the double deckers were usually hauled by two horses; double harness certainly still exists in the tramway stock, but it might have been used for training purposes with young horses. When tramcar 18 was restored to its former double-decked glory, therefore, there was much discussion about whether it would be cruel to use it with only one horse. The tramway operators compromised. On the rare occasions the double decker is used, only the top deck carries passengers (which they'd probably choose anyway); the lower deck remains empty.

Some visitors worry about whether the tram horses are overworked or ill treated. They are not. Not only would it be cruel, it also makes no economic sense to abuse animals on which your income or revenue depends. (Employers could take note here!) For a horse, well fed, fussed over, with enough work to do to be interesting but not so much that they become jaded, the rest of their herd for company in the stables, and most of the winter at grass, it must be a lovely life.

LESS OBSCURE

Made it! Phew!

Bill leaned on his stick and breathed deeply. Now he was here he didn't have to be in too much of a rush to unlock and set out the leaflets and what not. It wasn't as though they had a queue of visitors. He hadn't been volunteering to man the Camera Obscura for very long and he didn't want to get a reputation for not turning up. His colleague – um, Lucy something – had telephoned just as he was leaving to say that one of her children had fallen off a swing and had a suspected greenstick fracture. Could he cope on his own. Well, yes he could. He wasn't in his dotage yet and, although he didn't know as much about the mechanism as some of the volunteers (including Lucy), he probably knew enough to field most enquiries.

In fact it had been touch and go whether they opened the old Victorian building this afternoon. Wind and threatening rain meant few tourists would be likely to venture up Douglas Head. Still, visibility

The Great Union Camera Obscura on Douglas Head. Below to the left is the Douglas Head lighthouse. Incidentally, the camera obscura is not advertising real ale (CAMpaign for Real Ale); the missing 'e' is painted on a wall which the photographer can't see

was OK, no really low cloud, so he might get the odd visitor. Bill knew there was no point in opening up when Manannan's cloak covered Douglas Head. As part of his training he'd been shown the view from the Camera Obscura when it was misty and basically there wasn't one.

He unlocked the door, dealt with the burglar alarm and what not, and set the partitioning so that visitor could come in. He switched the light on – people were always surprised that they had electricity, but they had to have it to illuminate the emergency escape routes – and switched on the low level heat to air the place. He also swept up the leaves which had blown in with him; he wouldn't take his coat off for a bit. Then he did what he loved to do and went up to the inner gallery to open the shutters covering the lenses and raise the mirrors. the public weren't allowed up here and he still felt the thrill of someone allowed behind the scenes. Then he went back down to check what was happening outside. The inner room was dark and private and reminded him of the cinema with its air of mystery and expectation, but the moving picture show was endlessly varied. Wandering along the circular corridor he looked at the views on the eleven tables.

Once they knew he volunteered at the Camera Obscura once a month, lots of his friends asked him why they should pay to go inside to look at a view they could see from the headland for free, but they'd obviously never visited the Victorian attraction. It was as if the old lenses could isolate small dramatic events which, although visible, you probably wouldn't notice if you were gazing at the panorama. Kathy, his wife, had sniffed a little when he tried to explain it to her and commented tartly about it sounding like being a peeping Tom. He didn't tell her that, only the other day he'd seen the daughter of a friend of theirs steal a kiss from her boyfriend. Bob would be furious if he knew what his daughter was getting up to, but Bill just smiled. He remembered stealing a kiss in just the same way from Kathy when they'd both been sixteen, and they'd been married forty-six years.

He completed his circuit and unscrewed the top of his flask of hot water. Spooning instant coffee into the mug, and taking off his coat he settled down to wait for visitors.

An hour later he was still waiting. He'd never known it so quiet. OK, it wasn't a brilliant day, and the view was best on bright days, but it wasn't too bad. He got up from behind the desk and wondered whether he should prop the door open to encourage visitors, but the wind was blowing from just the wrong angle. Not only would he freeze, the leaflets would get blown about, and they'd also get all sorts of dust and leaves in. Besides light would ruin the pictures on the tables. He left the door closed and went back into the darkness of the table room to look at the view again.

ARRIVING AT DOUGLAS, I.O.M.

DOUGLAS HEAD.

The only movement was a young lad hurrying down the steps of the path which ran just behind the wooden building. Bill was about to move on to one of the other views when something caught his eye. The lad was carrying an old Shoprite bag – nothing strange about that – but he wasn't carrying it by the handles. It had been wrapped around something heavy which he was hugging to him. Bill bent closer and, using the flat of his hand, scooped part of the image off the table. Lifting it like this meant that he could enlarge it slightly, although the image went a bit fuzzy. His frowned in concentration. Then he dropped the young man back onto the Victorian screen and hurried over to his coat.

Sites and Stories

'So, Mr Taylor, what made you suspicious?' PC Kewin was sitting on one of the volunteers' chairs in the tiny ticket office as the wind battered the Victorian building; the weather had closed in and they'd get no more visitors today.

'He looked furtive,' Bill said, almost apologetically, 'and when I looked more closely, he seemed to be carrying something like a DVD player in an old plastic bag.' Kewin nodded. He forbore to tell the old chap that, far from being a DVD, it was actually a very expensive piece of recording kit which Manx Radio had reported had been lifted from one of their studios.

'Go on.'

'Well, my daughter bought me a mobile phone and made me promise to keep it with me.' Bill looked sheepish, 'I fell over in the house not so long ago, and she thinks that I'm getting past it. My wife was across visiting her sister and I didn't tell her that I'd had a mate round and we'd had a bit too much to drink.' Bill grinned slightly and the young constable joined him in a small male conspiracy:

'So you thought you'd give us a ring. Very good of you.' Kewin had been sent out to talk to the old man more in hope than expectation, but it might turn out useful after all. He started to ask about descriptions but Bill forestalled him:

'There's a bit more to it than that. My young granddaughter – she's only eight but all these youngsters have mobiles – showed me how to take photographs on it.' Kewin looked up sharply. 'So I did. Not of him you understand, but of the image of him on the table. It's not very good, but it might help?' Kewin nodded quickly and held out his hand:

'May I have the phone, sir?' Bill handed it over with an air of taking no responsibility for it. He did however look on interestedly as Kewin, with the ease of a proficient, identified the pictures, accessed them and peered at the tiny screen. He also didn't miss the look of satisfaction on the constable's face.

'I didn't like to go out and accost him,' Bill went on. 'Apart from the fact I wouldn't have

Interior of camera obscura. Left: Douglas Head projected onto one of the eleven tables. Below: the circular corridor and one of the tables showing the steps outside the front door

been able to catch him, I get a bit breathless.' Kewin nodded. It was just as well the old boy hadn't gone out. He knew this young man very well and they'd been trying to prove something against him for some time. He was the sort who'd have knocked Bill down and hit him with his own walking stick if he thought he'd seen anything. The island didn't have a lot of crime, but most of it seemed to be caused by Barry Howard and his mates.

'Can I use your phone to make a call?' Bill was surprised:

'Sure.' He was even more surprised when, rather than actually talking to anyone, Kewin sent the pictures back to the station. 'That's neat. Can you teach me how it's done, then I can show off to the grandkids?' Grinning the young policeman showed him. As he demonstrated Kewin said:

'You say he didn't know you were here?'

'I'm sure he didn't.'

'We might be able to pick him up with the stuff still on him then. If you're really sure?'

Bill looked embarrassed. 'I'm sure,' he said, rubbing the back of his head, 'I haven't been volunteering at the Camera Obscura for very long. I…er… well, with all the stuff I had to do I forgot to hang out the flag.'

'What flag?' Constable Kewin was only mildly curious.

'The Manx flag that hangs outside next to the door. We always say, if the flag is flying we're open for visitors. People can see it from down the cliff you see, so know whether to bother coming up the hill or not. I, er, forgot. So no-one came. I thought it had been a bit quiet…'

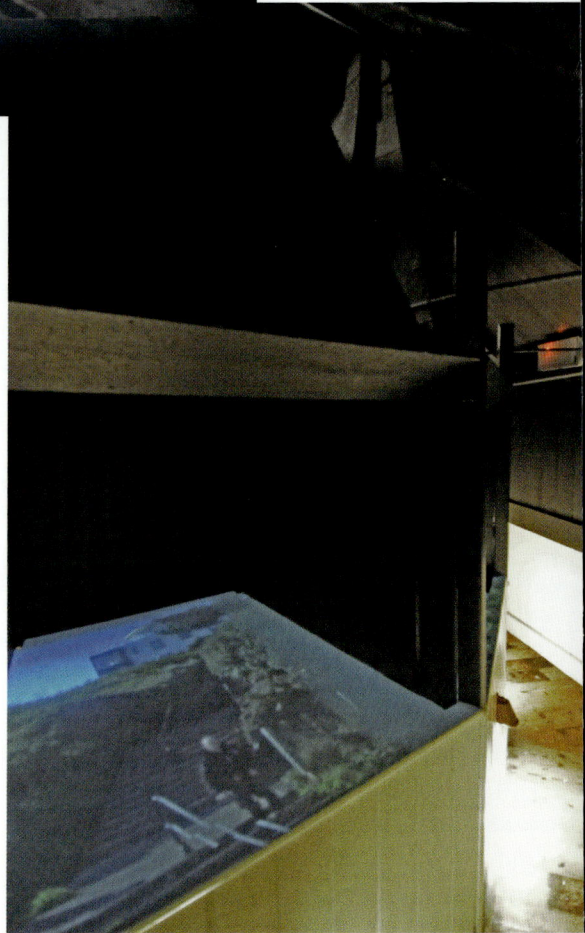

ELEGANTLY OLD FASHIONED

It might look relatively deserted now, but at the end of the nineteenth century Douglas Head was a magnet for tourists. In addition to the hotel, which had accommodation but was largely designed to cater for the huge numbers of visitors, Douglas Head had toboggan slides, an inclined railway, the route of which can still clearly be seen, an open-air theatre, the remnants of which are again clearly visible and Punch and Judy shows. A steam ferry carried a small orchestra and the Douglas Southern Electric Tramway providing what must have been a thrilling tram ride along the Marine Drive to Port Soderick.

So popular was Douglas Head with visitors, that the same company which owned the Marine Drive tramway proposed to build a direct link with the southern end of Loch Promenade via a suspension bridge over the harbour. Different plans had been proposed for such a connexion, via bridge or tunnel, for most of the 1880s. A ceremonial laying of the foundation stone for the bridge (roughly where the Sea Terminal is now) had even taken place on 24 October 1890. The money soon ran out, however, and, within a couple of years, the bridge plan was abandoned. Even so, the numbers of visitors taking the air and enjoying the amenities of Douglas Head meant that the more modest and private speculation of constructing a camera obscura had a much greater chance of success.

The first camera obscura on Douglas Head was built in the early 1880s. It was owned and operated by Mr Hicks, who also lived in it, so was unfortunately made homeless when it burned down in 1887. The current building

dates probably from 1892. John Richard Fielding applied for the patent to build the camera obscura, but he may not actually have owned it, as there are reports in the local press of the time referring to it as 'Mr Williams' Camera Obscura'. Press reports may or may not be accurate of course. In its original form the camera obscura was a virtually round building with no entrance lobby and, very unusually had twelve lenses.

Camerae obscurae work a little like periscopes with one or more lenses reflecting the view outside via a mirror onto a table in a darkened room below – the name camera obscura is derived from the Latin *camera* meaning room (English gets the word chamber from the same root) and *obscura* meaning dark or – obviously – obscure. Most camerae obscurae had a single lens set in a revolving turret which an operator turned by means of a handle to point at

different aspects of the view outside. Visitors group around the table below to look at whatever the lens is pointing at. Naturally, as the lens is rotated to look at different aspects outside, the image it displays will also rotate, so some visitors around a central table will see it upside down. Occasionally, if there is only an interesting view one way – if the camera obscura were set against a cliff for example – one or more lenses can be fixed, thus obviating the need for a handle-turning operator, but giving a fixed view one way. The Douglas Head camera obscura is unique in that it provides a 360° view using only fixed lenses. It also has the advantage over single-lens camerae obscurae in that its receiving tables – one for each lens – are set out in a circle so that, as visitors walk round, all the views are seen the correct way up.

The idea of seeing without being seen must have been very popular as, in 1896, the same year that the Douglas Southern Electric Tramway opened just up the hill, the small box office was built to improve the flow of visitors round the viewing tables and through the building. Rumours have suggested that one reason for the Douglas Head camera obscura's popularity was the proximity of the Port Skillion bathing pool on the small beach below the attraction. Built by Robert Archer in 1874 a series of concrete walls trapped sea water at high tide and provided

deep water sea bathing free of charge regardless of the state of the tide. The pool was, however, for men only, some of whom, particularly in its early days, swam without the benefit of bathing costume. Women could not walk the cliff paths and look at the scene without possible damage to their reputation, although there were complaints about some shameless hussies who did. Visiting the camera obscura, however, was quite respectable…

Construction of the box office blocked the projected image from the inland-facing lens immediately above the entrance, so the Great Union Camera Obscura, to give it its full title, currently has eleven working lenses. From outside visitors can clearly see the eleven lenses emerging from the roof of the building, housed under small dormer roofs. The small door covering each window is raised by a cord from inside the building. A second cord positions the mirror so that the picture projected by the lens is angled onto the trapeze-shaped table below. The twelfth dormer was never removed as to do so would spoil the exterior symmetry and charm of the building. Visitors can easily tell which it is, however, as, unlike the others, the aperture is not uncovered when the camera obscura is in use. Having only eleven lenses when twelve were intended means that the view inside is not quite a complete circle, although almost so; the view from each lens overlaps that of its immediate neighbour slightly.

In 1907 the camera obscura was sold to John Heaton. A former employee of John Fielding, who patented the camera obscura, Mr Heaton seems to have branched out on his own. The little building remained in the Heaton family for over eighty years, but gradually fell into decay as Douglas Head became less popular with tourists.

In the early 1990s the Isle of Man government purchased the Victorian attraction to ensure that it could be saved to entertain future generations. Until they could devote the funds to its restoration, a corrugated iron shed was built around the camera obscura, partly to protect it from the elements and partly to deter vandals and fire raisers. The old building dozed in its tin hut for nearly ten years until it was reopened to the public in 2005 after being lovingly restored by APA Architects. The Great Union Camera Obscura is one of only eight working camerae obscurae in the British Isles – the others are at Brighton, Bristol, Eastbourne and Greenwich in England, Dumfries and Edinburgh in Scotland and Aberystwyth in Wales – and is the only one to have eleven lenses.

Today the camera obscura is staffed by The Victorian Society who man it on a voluntary basis at weekends and bank holidays during the summer and who welcome several thousand visitors to it each year. The volunteers on duty announce that the attraction is open to visitors by flying a Manx flag from the flagpole just outside the box office; no flag, no admittance. The labourers who built the Victorian camera obscura, many of whom may not have been able to read, would probably have approved of the beautifully simple idea.

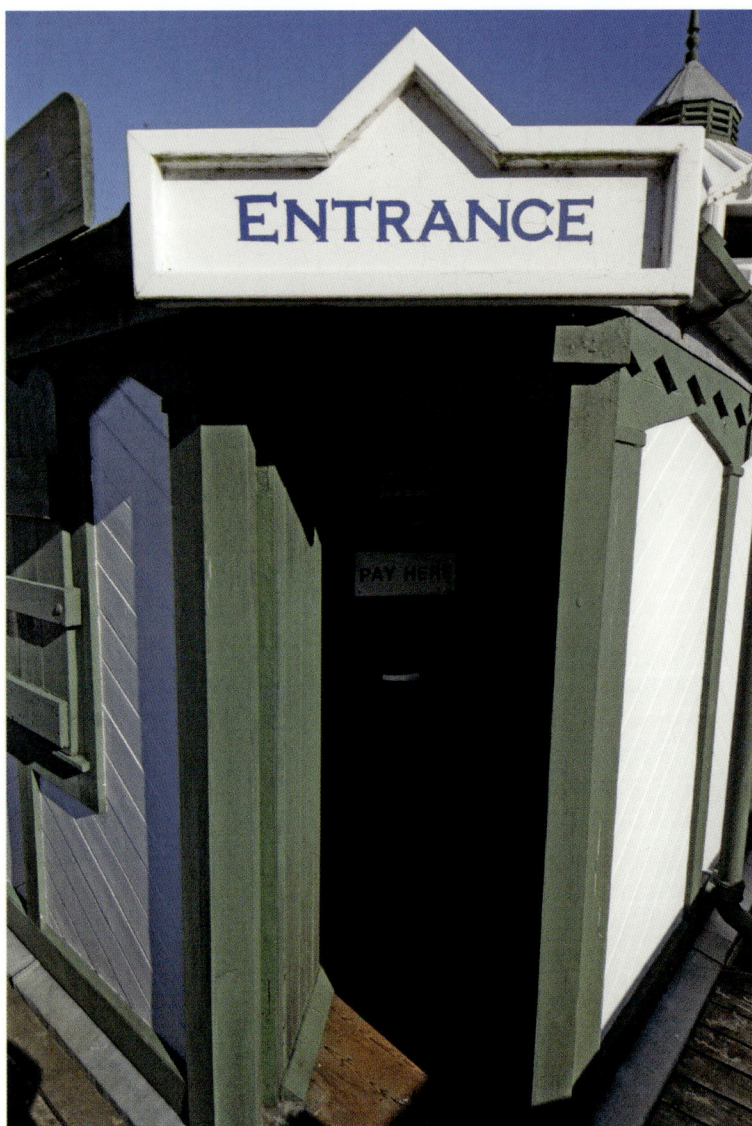

Sites and Stories

MERRY WANDERER OF THE NIGHT*

And where, may I ask, are… er… Themselves?'
Everyone knew he meant the fairies. No-one laughed at his attempt to avoid bad luck by not naming them. Assorted oddly-dressed people milled about, most of them ignoring the man with the clipboard. He looked round distractedly and then beckoned energetically:

'Helena! *Helena!*' A middle-aged woman in a long dress and a rather obvious wig pushed her way out of the crowd. She looked both startled and huffy:

'Helena, I thought one of your grandchildren was a fairy. Where's she got to?'

'My name's Kathy.' He felt the comment to be supremely irrelevant.

'You're playing Helena aren't you?' As the woman began an excited exposition about her reading of the part, Mike Cowin ran his fingers through his hair. Why, oh why had he agreed to get involved with this farce? It had been a problem from the start. And it had sounded like such a good idea: the local amateur dramatic group doing an outdoor performance in Peel Castle to raise money for Manx National Heritage. The Manannan Players were enthusiastic. They'd chosen their play, had it and the venue agreed and were going ahead with auditions, when an office transfer to Cardiff had whisked away their director. Mike had been dragooned in as one of those temporary stop gaps which somehow becomes permanent. He did hope they weren't being too ambitious.

He ran his fingers through his hair again. Over on the Bowling Green he heard a mock-terrified scream and saw half a dozen gaudily-dressed fairies in a whispering huddle. Queen

* A Midsummer Night's Dream Act II, Sc i, L 43

Peel castle, looking towards the town. The building in the foreground was once a kitchen, the partially ruined building behind it is the second hall; St German's cathedral is at the back on the right

Elizabeth II High School had obliged with keen youngsters. He really was *not* prepared to have Mrs Pertwee prancing about the greensward as an ageing nymph. Fortunately Mrs Pertwee, eighteen stone and sixty, totally agreed with him. She was playing Philostrate, Master of the Revels – and why not? She was a jovial, friendly, thoroughly nice woman ideally suited to revel-organising. He called:

'Cobweb! Peaseblossom! Come on you lot, this is supposed to be a dress rehearsal – we're on tonight.' Giggling they scurried over.

'I thought there were only five of you? Oh, well, never mind – a couple of you under the arcades, the rest in the half moon battery.' Rather than have the audience raised around the action, he'd decided to have the action above and among the audience. It had sounded such a good idea, bringing in, as it did, the remains of St German's cathedral as a magical backdrop and utilising the gatehouse as well as the grass in front of the armoury. Now he wasn't so sure. It demanded a lot from his actors, not least the strain of making themselves heard. As the fairies pushed and giggled away, he thought, with the part of his brain which wasn't counting courtiers, organising the prompt and worrying about the seating, that 'wardrobe' – Mrs Quemby and various friends from the WI – had done them proud with the costumes. The wings on the small fairy at the back looked big enough to trip her up, but they were remarkably realistic. He said, for what must have been the seventh time:

'Places everyone, we'll take it from the top.'

As he listened to the opening lines of the play, he fervently hoped… for what? His amateurs to turn into Stratford professionals? The obvious drawbacks to look like a deliberately sideways slant on a well-known play? He grinned to himself – he'd settle for everything happening in the right place and without a hitch. Fiddling with his hair yet again, Mike realised that he'd developed this nervous trick because he wasn't used to having so much of it. The tawny wig

Sites and Stories

framed his face like a lion's mane but, in an odd sort of way, suited him. It certainly added to Oberon's impressive dignity. Or at least Mike hoped it did.

He'd wanted Oberon to be played by someone imposing. Not only would the character contrast tellingly with the dainty wisp of tulle who was playing Titania, but it would emphasise all the things words such as 'fairy' tended to destroy. Right from the outset he'd tried to avoid all the limp-wristed jokes, camp comments and mincing innuendos. He'd stressed the fact that Oberon was a Mighty King, that he was Linked with Mystic Powers, and was probably an Alpha Male as well. The capital letters had made no difference. The Manannan Players were keen, enthusiastic, and almost entirely female. Several of the ladies were eager to take the role, but Mike wouldn't have that. It wasn't panto they were doing, it was Shakespeare, he'd said. In Shakespeare's time most people believed in fairies and were, if anything, frightened of them, he'd said. He wanted to bring back some of that mystique, he'd said. He'd said! He'd had to compromise of course. The rude mechanicals were female to a man. So was the Master of the Revels, and, more disturbingly, Hermia's father. When 'King of the Fairies' was mentioned, the comments of the three men he'd managed to shanghai into the

![St German's cathedral looking north. The two buttress-like sections of wall in the foreground are the sanctuary pillars](image)

St German's cathedral looking north. The two buttress-like sections of wall in the foreground are the sanctuary pillars

play were caustic in the extreme. Then of course someone suggested him. He sighed again. It was true that, at six foot three, he was the only one with the height to dominate anything, but his build was more beanstalk than beefcake. Perhaps the costume would help…

After the late start the dress rehearsal went surprisingly well. As the play unwound, Mike made mental notes about necessary improvements. The twenty-year old duke with his forty-year old bride looked incongruous but, well, there were such things as political marriages and anyway Hippolyta's acting carried them through. The fairies were unusually giggly and one didn't seem to have any dialogue, but there were directions for 'fairy attendants' so perhaps they'd found a few. The rude mechanicals were the undoubted stars of the play. They were stunningly good, managing to tread the fine line between hilarity and embarrassment. The problems he'd feared with the woman pretending to be a man pretending to be a woman just hadn't materialised. The happy ending rolled out, the fairies blessed the various marriages and fifteen-year-old Puck stepped forward to speak the epilogue. Framed by the sanctuary pillars she was extraordinary, thought Mike, captured by the moment. Miraculously *A Midsummer*

Night's Dream had drawn the band of unlikely thespians into its spell. Puck was quiveringly still, a secret smile playing on her face:

'Give me your hands if we be friends…' As she darted away, the tawdry sequins on her costume lent her a flash of fairy light.

Mike pulled off his itching wig and sighed in relief. Perhaps there really was something in this 'it'll be alright on the night' business:

'OK, everyone, gather round, just one or two things…'

The small fairy with the huge wings looked down from the top of the round tower. He too did the equivalent of sigh. It had all been very odd. This posting was far more complicated than the ministry had led him to believe. The embassy was OK, if a bit cramped under that bridge, and he had learned a lot, but it had been a huge strain trying to blend in. Still… Unnoticed he fluttered down inside the great hall. They'd arranged to pick him up here. Tonight. He'd hand over to his replacement and then he'd get to go home. It was a long way to Proxima Centauri. Until then there was that nice black dog to play with…

TWO SAINTS AND A CASTLE

Situated on St Patrick's Isle, the ruins of Peel Castle still dominate the harbour. From the town the gatehouse is most prominent, but viewed from the sea, the imposing curtain wall still provides a barrier to unwanted visitors, as it has for over five hundred years. The wall's construction began in the middle of the fifteenth century when two Thomases, Thomas Stanley, First Earl of Derby and King of Man, and his son also called Thomas wanted to fortify the existing castle. The curtain wall connected up the flanking fourteenth century towers, and so linked some of the existing fortifications in a wall which enclosed many earlier buildings. The oldest remaining of these is the tenth century round tower. There are over seventy such towers left in Britain, and the sites of a further thirty are known, although the towers themselves don't survive. Almost all are in Ireland. The three exceptions are the one on St Patrick's Isle and one each at Brechin and Abernethy in Scotland.

St Patrick's Isle was inhabited long before even the round tower was built, however. Judging by flint fragments found under the half-moon battery, the island's first visitors arrived about 6,000 BC, although the first people to live there rather than merely visiting it to fish or hunt, probably arrived around five thousand years later. From around 1,000 BC archaeological finds indicate that the island was home to several generations of farming community. In 450 BC they left behind them the earliest human flea to be found in Britain.

St Patrick's Isle is traditionally the site where the Irish saint first set foot on the Isle of Man bringing Christianity to the Manx, and is, of course, where the island of Peel Castle gets its name. Until the causeway was built in the mid eighteenth century St Patrick's island was separated from the town by a narrow strait walkable at low tide. In Manx, Peel is *Purt ny hInchen*, which means 'port of the island', the island being St Patrick's Isle rather than the mainland of Mann. The town's English name stems from its castle. Peel or pele castles were fortified towers used as watch towers and for defence, and where the local ruler would live; they are particularly common in Scotland. Peel Castle is a bit big to be classed as a true peel or pele castle, but the combination of observation post, defence and accommodation is almost certainly where the name come from.

The causeway which now joins St Patrick's Isle to the Manx mainland began life as a breakwater to protect the town of Peel, but soon became established as a useful land crossing. The strip of sand to the south of the causeway is known as Fenella Beach after the daughter of Edward Christian in Sir Walter Scott's novel *Peveril of the Peak*. The book features the Stanley family who ruled Mann for over three hundred years, and is set largely in England although it contains several Manx references and a brief visit to Peel Castle.

With St Patrick being such an important figure in Manx religious history it seems odd that both the ruined cathedral on St Patrick's Isle, and its replacement at Derby Road, Peel, are dedicated to St German and not the Irish saint. St German is rather elusive with at least two men apparently eligible for the title. The cathedral itself claims that its patron saint is St German of Man, also known as Noo Carmane, who was born in Brittany and went to Ireland to stay with St Patrick. He is occasionally credited as becoming Bishop of Man in 466, but as the first Bishop of Man is generally considered to be Roolwer, who was appointed around 1050, Carmane's claim may be weaker than it appears. The other and slightly earlier St German is St Germanus of Auxerre who visited Britain twice and one of whose disciples was St Patrick. Many scholars in fact consider the two saints to be the same person but, whoever he was, he was treated with some deference by the Manx as not only the island's cathedral, but also the parish which encompasses the area around Peel, is named after him. To be even handed, a neighbouring parish is named Patrick, as is a smaller and older church, built in the eleventh century, on St Patrick's Isle.

The cathedral is one of the largest and most complete of the ruined buildings within the outer wall of the castle. It was completed in the thirteenth century by Simon, the first Bishop of Sodor and Man to be accepted as such by all branches of the church. The sanctuary pillars, south west of the cathedral, have nothing to do with the area of the cathedral building known as the sanctuary where the altar is situated. They are in fact the remains of a gateway and mark where a wall used to run around the cathedral precinct. From the fourth to the seventeenth century the right of sanctuary was part of common law and usually but not invariably connected with churches. Most churches for most of that period could extend sanctuary to those who claimed it, provided they stayed within the church building. Some churches – and St German's Cathedral appears to be one of these – were granted a charter to extend their sanctuary area beyond the church building. Such an area, if small, could be encompassed within a wall, as appears to be the case at St German's; if the sanctuary was more extensive its boundary was marked with crosses. Accused persons could claim sanctuary for usually around 40 days – the exact number of days varied according to period and geography – if they reached the sanctuary area before being caught. Although it sounds anachronistic, peasants couldn't appeal to law to have overturned accusations levied by their overlords, and sanctuary was often their only recourse against injustice.

Originally a religious foundation and containing the Isle of Man's cathedral, St Patrick's Isle had long been recognised as equally important for defence. Secular and religious interests therefore clashed. Magnus III of Norway, known as Magnus Barelegs, built a fortified hall on the small island early in the eleventh century. For the next couple of centuries the castle grew piecemeal and included the Lord's House which adjoined the cathedral to the north, the Gatehouse, with red sandstone flanking walls to protect the island from attack from the town, and the Warwick Tower, named after the Earl of Warwick who was imprisoned there in 1398. The whole was surrounded by a bank topped by a log palisade. This in turn was replaced by the curtain wall which appears to have been built into the front of the existing bank.

St Patrick's Isle is basically a very large grass-covered rock in the Irish sea, so little of it is flat. The biggest levelled area, in the western part of the island, was used as a bowling green in the sixteenth and seventeenth centuries, but started life as an archery field. Mediaeval sappers clearing and levelling the ground, piled up the spoil into heaps on the three sides of the ground away from the sea. Arrows fired by novice or over-enthusiastic archers which missed the target would be safely buried in the

earth banks. Later the same area was used for musket practice.

The Isle of Man is rich in stories about fairies, although the Manx think it rude to call them such, preferring to talk about them obliquely as 'Themselves'. Several parishes claim to have a Fairy Bridge, although the most famous is the one over Santon Burn on the A5 between Ronaldsway airport and Douglas. When crossing the bridge, tradition exhorts everyone to greet the fairies with a wave. Residents who fail to do so will have bad luck, and visitors to the island who don't wave won't be allowed to visit again. Themselves dislike discourtesy.

Peel Castle doesn't have any particular connexion with fairies, at least not more than most places on Mann, but it does have its own supernatural inhabitant. The *Moddey Dhoo* (pronounced, roughly, Maw-tha Doo) is a large black dog said to haunt the dark passages leading to the guard room of the castle. The story was first recorded by George Waldron in the 1720s, although it dates from sixty years earlier. During the English Civil War, Peel Castle was still a working fortification and heavily guarded, first by factions loyal to the crown and then by ruling parliamentarians. It continued to be garrisoned after the restoration of the monarchy in Britain and the rule of the Stanley family in Mann.

As is usual in any building needing to be kept secure, the guards had particular routines for handling keys and delivering them to the captain of the guard. To hand over the keys securely guards had to walk along a dark passageway to the guard room. The corridor led through one of the old chapels, the building of which predated the castle. Time and again they saw a large black dog trotting noiselessly along the passage. With its hair bristling and its eyes glowing red, it entered the guard's room and sat or lay by the fire until just before dawn when it left just as soundlessly. Its unearthly presence kept the soldiers unusually restrained and respectful and none would walk alone at night.

On a night of celebration, however, one soldier had drunk too deeply before (and perhaps during) his time on duty. Filled with liquor-induced courage he boasted that he would see whether the beast was dog or devil, seized the keys and ventured into the passage alone. The silence grew until it was broken by unearthly screams and howls. Minutes later the soldier returned, silent, sober and staring. His face was silvery and twisted with fear and he refused to eat, sleep or speak. For three days he existed like an automaton. On the fourth day he died.

The Peel Castle soldiers could take no more and sealed off the haunted passageway, breaking through a new access to the guard room which avoided the Moddey Dhoo's domain. It is said that the dog has never appeared since.

But, who knows?...

Sites and Stories

THE LADY IN THE LAKE

The elderly woman was distressed. She was overweight, her face was mottled and she had obviously been running far faster than was good for her. The staff at the entrance to the wildlife park hurried to her aid:

'There's someone…' the woman tried to catch her breath. Various people began to make soothing noises, offer a chair, a glass of water. She waved them away impatiently:

'A woman, in the lake,' she gasped again, 'I think she's drowning.'

Everyone froze. Then everyone spoke at once:

'Which lake? Which one? We've several…' The woman held up her hand:

'The… the one… near the otters.'

The North American Trail. The staff swung into action as though people in lakes were commonplace (they weren't) and as though they'd been rehearsing regularly how to deal with the unexpected (they had). The emergency services were contacted, keepers sent off with floats and ropes and, with some prescience, the Park Manager rang the press office at the government's Department of Community, Culture and Leisure. Amid the whirl of purposeful activity, Mrs Cunningham finally allowed herself to sink into the offered chair. A very young shop assistant, left behind among the soft toys, stayed with her in case she needed comforting. She didn't.

Mrs Cunningham was a personality. Determinedly good-humoured, forcibly kind, alarmingly efficient. A nice woman though, everyone said so, although no-one got so close that they needed to find out. She eyed her awed companion and offered a mischievous and surprisingly youthful grin:

'If I said that I could do with a cup of tea, do you think I'd have to pay for it?' Tracy Quayle was startled into giggles:

'Don't 'spect so. I'll get you one.' The police and an ambulance arrived at the same time as the tea. By the time they'd viewed the body – dragged out of the lake by assorted bystanders – ascertained that the woman was beyond help, found out from the staff what had happened and returned hot foot to the

shop to make sure that Mrs Cunningham had not disappeared, she and the Tracy were on their second cup of tea and were postulating wilder and wilder theories about how the woman got into the lake. Sergeant McDowell interrupted, rather brusquely:

'You found the body?' Mrs Cunningham switched off her smile and stared imperiously up at the sergeant. Brusqueness never worked with her:

'No, I found a woman floundering in the lake.' The sergeant blinked, but before he could recover Mrs Cunningham continued, 'presumably help wasn't quick enough? She's dead?' Reaching for her walking stick she added, 'you'll want a statement. Where should I go?' Tracy, charmed into partisanship, took her cup and glared rather unfairly at the sergeant.

As it was, Mrs Cunningham needn't have been hurried. Two young men who had tried to help the 'lady in the lake' as the local press were to call her, were being taken away in the otherwise redundant ambulance for a routine hospital check up which probably included various inoculations. Trevor Link and Matthew Kneale were about eighteen, looked, for the moment at least, much younger, and were trying to hide their shock under a precariously nonchalant shell. They were sitting in the back of the ambulance, wrapped in blankets, as Inspector Babcock leaned in to talk to them. Matthew, who was soaked as well as shocked, was shivering:

'Sure,' he said through chattering teeth, 'we heard someone scream and then a splash. Didn't take any notice, though – just thought it was people larking about.' Trevor nodded, but kept his head down. Sergeant McDowell was watching him sharply. The lad spoke hurriedly:

'When we got there we saw some old biddy in the duckpond and another one going tarzan in the trees. Matt went in and I went to get the float thing. By the time I got back he'd staggered out again saying it was too muddy and he couldn't get to her. Well, look at him,' he jerked his head, 'he's covered with the stuff.' Swallowing he added, 'I had a couple of goes at chucking the float but the granny in the pond wouldn't grab it. She'd gone really still…' Matthew wrapped his blanket closer around him and offered:

'It warn't deep, but real slippery. The other old fossil went for help and we thought she'd be ages…,' his teeth resumed chattering and Trevor took over again:

'She was quick, though. People started arriving – two in a boat and two more with long poles on the bank. Then the biddy in the pool started to sink…' his voice trailed off and, without warning, Matthew was suddenly sick:

'Sorry,' he mumbled, wiping his mouth on the back of his hand and looking in distress at the mess on the blanket. The medics intervened:

'Scuse us, mate,' one of them said to Inspector Babcock and firmly closed the ambulance door. As the frustrated inspector watched the vehicle disappear, siren wailing, his sergeant cleared his throat:

'I know those two, sir. At least I know the dark one, Trevor Link.' Babcock gave him a sharp glance and McDowell continued: 'he's been in trouble for nicking stuff from gift shops…'

The interview with Mrs Cunningham was a much more leisurely and thorough affair. With the agreement of the manager, it was conducted in a corner of the Lakeside Café, fortunately not overlooking the lake now cordoned off, but over the display showing a flooded Amazon forest. Herded into a private corner away from curious visitors Mrs Cunningham, Sergeant McDowell and Inspector Babcock huddled in almost embarrassing proximity. Mrs Cunningham was white but composed. Without fuss, she provided her name and address but, when asked why she was visiting the Curraghs Wildlife Park, was obviously taken aback:

'Well, because it's here,' she said, with bewildered honesty, 'I just… well, fancied doing something a bit different.' Her face darkened in apparent distress, 'I've certainly done that…' In response to Inspector Babcock's quiet questioning she told him she'd been looking at the wildlife in the Australian section and had hurried along the path on hearing the scream and

splash. She'd seen a woman struggling in the water in what looked like a heavyish coat:

'The coat was getting sodden and muddy and I think there were weeds too. She obviously couldn't swim and kept slipping. I hurried down to the edge of the path – the rail had been broken so I held on to one of the trees while I reached out with my walking stick. She seemed to be making grabs for it, but kept floundering out of reach.' Mrs Cunningham looked up at the inspector and said with a slightly defiant directness:

'I've been blaming myself. Thinking that I should have perhaps gone further… I don't know… waded in…' Inspector Babcock shook his head firmly:

'No, Mrs Cunningham. The keepers say that it's very marshy just there and the footing is probably very treacherous. If you'd ventured in we might have had two bodies to fish out of the pond.' She flinched slightly and he, looking at her muddy shoes, splashed coat and soggy stick, added kindly: 'You did your best.'

'Yes, well…' Mrs Cunningham looked down at her linked fingers for a moment, composed herself and went on:

'As I was swinging about at the end of the branch, trying to reach out with my stick, I heard footsteps running along the path behind me. A couple of young men came up, I don't really know where from. They started shouting things…'

'Rude things?' interrupted Sergeant McDowell. His experience of young lads shouting things had usually involved bad language, abuse and occasionally violence.

'No, oh no. Instructions really. One shouted that he'd go for the lifebelt, the other told me to fetch help… Really,' she paused, almost amused at herself, 'I'm not used to being ordered about like that. In fact,' she added candidly, 'it's usually me doing the ordering, but he was quite right. I watched him try and wade after the woman – she wasn't struggling so much by that time – and then ran to get help. There wasn't anyone in the Rainforest Theatre and I didn't think about this place.' She glanced around without really seeing the counter, spectators or view, and added musingly, 'Stupid really… not like me. Anyway I ran back to the entrance. And,' she added firmly, 'I really shouldn't be running at my time of life…'

While Mrs Cunningham was being brushed down by a solicitous Tracy and then taken home by an equally solicitous PC, the inspector

investigated the contents of the dead woman's handbag. None of the three people directly involved with the abortive rescue had said they'd known her, but, to his surprise, the gardeners did. One of them, a student working during his vacation from horticultural college, was obviously trying to temper his indignation with suitable reverence for the dead:

'Her name's Clarissa Martin, inspector, and she was a regular visitor, a life member I think. I'd been told to keep an eye on her if I spotted her, because she pinched cuttings. It doesn't sound much, but, if everyone did it, the shrubs would look a real mess. Besides, they're valuable and we'd have nothing suitable left for our own use – some of these hardy hybrids are quite rare.' Dodging the horticultural details the inspector mentally filed the death as a tragic accident. One of the ambulance men had mentioned a head injury which looked as though the woman had hit her head on a branch. The inspector didn't know a sycamore from a sequoia, so if the woman had been straining to reach cuttings from the rarer plants…

After work, Tracy made her way to the hospital:
'Matt's being kept in overnight,' Trevor said as he kissed her.
'Funny you being involved,' she said, 'I suppose you didn't get what you wanted?'
'Just as well. That nosy copper recognised me. Still, I can tell you something funny. That fence what was broken. It's really sturdy and that was a new break – me and Matt heard the crack as it went. That biddy must have bust it to jump in on purpose…'

Back in her own garden Mrs Cunningham replaced the rubber ferrule on the bottom of her walking stick. As she had thought, before she struck, the wooden stick left no mark which could be identified. There were plenty of trees about. Pushing someone under was certainly much easier than trying to fish them out. She considered the forthcoming horticultural show. After a decade of running up, this year she'd be bound to win the cup for the best roses. Now that Mrs Martin was out of the way.

Near Close Beg is the station for the Orchid Line, named after the heath spotted orchids which grow in profusion in the wetland. The Close Startfield nature reserve, where hay meadows are managed by the Manx Wildlife Trust, shares the Ballaugh Curraghs with the wildlife park. Just as bluebells turn the woodland floor blue in May, early June sees the profusion of orchids turn meadows in Close Startfield pink in one of the finest displays of orchids in Europe. Sussex in England has its Bluebell Railway, the Isle of Man its Orchid Line. Opened in 1992, the Orchid Line is a multi-gauge miniature railway run by the Manx Model Engineering Society. Miniature steam, diesel or electric trains haul 'sit-astride' passenger carriers for a ride of about half a mile over bridges and through a tunnel. Operated by volunteers the Orchid Line runs on Sunday and bank holiday afternoons and provides a unique view of the Curragh wetland.

Possibly some of the most interesting exhibits – and the most appropriate from the Manx point of view – concern animal life on islands. While wildlife on the Isle of Man is very similar to that in the UK, there are distinct differences brought about by the fact that Mann is indeed an island entire of itself, at least in this case*. The Isle of Man lacks deer, moles, snakes, squirrels and badgers – and foxes are also largely unknown apart from a few which were imported illegally in the 1980s and whose offspring still survive here and there. The island also lacks some of the more common woodland birds such as jays and woodpeckers, which seems surprising until you see photographs of the island taken only a few decades ago. Tree cover, now so abundant, was much scarcer then. Life on islands therefore frequently evolves differently as a result of isolation, as the Isle of Man's own Manx cat clearly demonstrates.

Such island-bred animals and birds are often also more vulnerable as any intrusion on their isolation can endanger the balanced existence of island species. Again the wildlife park can talk from Manx experience as the Manx shearwater, a sea bird which raises its young in burrows, used to nest in their thousands on the Calf of Man. They were largely wiped out, partly because brown rats were accidentally introduced to the island and partly because the birds formed a welcome addition to the Manx crofters' diet and were easy to catch.

Using its own island status as a starting point the wildlife park emphasises the risk to

* Apologies to John Donne:
'No man is an island entire of itself;
every man is a piece of the continent,
a part of the main.'

other animals on other islands. Among a variety of island species, visitors can see lemurs from Madagascar, Hawaiian geese, Cuban boas and peacock pheasants from Palawan Island in the Philippines. The Bali Starling is pure white with a bright blue mask across its eyes and very attractive to collectors. Fewer than ten birds survive in the wild. The Curragh wildlife park is part of an international breeding programme to ensure that the bird can be reintroduced once numbers have grown – and once the education programme discouraging the birds' capture has been successful.

One very special island species is the Rodrigues Island Fruit Bat, sometimes known as the Rodrigues Flying Fox. It is a very special experience to walk through the large aviary in which the bats fly free. They are beautiful animals, but, be warned, for bats they are *very* large. An adult male can have a wingspan of almost a metre. If you're lucky enough to see them fly – they're largely nocturnal and don't fly much during the day – it's a really impressive sight. Once teetering on the brink of extinction, captive breeding programmes begun by the Jersey Wildlife Preservation Trust, but continued by organisations such as the Curragh Wildlife Park, have ensured that these gorgeous animals have been successfully reintroduced to the wild.

Access to the wildlife park is off the A3 road, which is squeezed between the wetland and the hill, Gob y Volley. Until it closed in 1968 the Manx Northern Railway ran close to and parallel with the road at this point. The railway connected Ramsey and St John's via a coastal route and had a siding and small goods yard connecting with a tiny branch line which served Clark's stone quarry situated part way up Gob y Volley. The quarry specialised in producing stone lintels for doors, windows and fireplaces, and is remembered in the name Quarry Bends on the TT course which runs along the A3 road at this point. More importantly from the wildlife park's point of view, the quarry's loading bay and siding off the railway line now forms the visitor's car park.

While not perhaps as exotic as more famous zoos, the Curragh Wildlife Park allows visitors to mingle with the animals in a way which larger zoos might envy. It is well worth a visit.

TIME ENOUGH

Today's the day! Ever since he moved to the island, which, OK, was when he was three, he'd intended to walk from Laxey harbour to the summit of Snaefell. It would be like taking his freedom of the place. And today he was going to do it.

He'd breakfasted early – his Mum had insisted on him eating properly 'for fuel' and – boring – had been around to ensure that he did. Then he'd donned his battered trainers, picked up the carrier bag containing his sandwiches and scooted past King Orry's grave down Cronk Vinorca, to the sea. Mr Crellin was working on his boat and Mike had waved at him:

'*Moghrey mie*, young Michael. So it's today is it?'

'Er… *moghrey mie* … er … *Benainstyr* Crellin,' Mike stumbled a bit over the Manx greeting and switched to English, 'yes, Mr Crellin, it's today.' The elderly man – he must be fifty at least – smiled kindly:

'Your Manx is coming on, Michael, but you've just called me *Mrs* Crellin. *Mainstyr* Crellin it should be.' Mike blushed, wished he hadn't, and stammered an apology.

'Oh, not to worry lad you'll learn, *traa dy liooar*. You know what that means?'

'Yes Mr Crellin, "time enough".' The man waved and wished him luck. Or at least Mike hoped that was what the Manx meant.

He walked resolutely down to the sea and dabbled his trainers in the edge of the water. If he managed to do the whole walk – he had to buy a postcard in the hotel on Snaefell summit to prove it – his Dad had promised to buy him some proper walking boots. Once his feet stopped growing.

Galloping feet on the shingle, six galloping feet to be precise, heralded the arrival of Lisa and her Labrador, Tilly:

'Today is it?' Lisa asked, out of puff. Tilly wambled up to him. It was their own term for the mix of waddling and gambolling which was the speciality of Labradors.

'Yes.' He concentrated fiercely on getting just the right amount of seawater on his trainers, as though it was a special benediction. And to avoid looking at her. He liked Lisa. And he liked Tilly. But he didn't want their company today.

'Bye then,' he said and risked a glance at her. She looked a bit disappointed, but not too much:

'Good luck,' she called. 'You've got lots of time. *Traa dy liooar.*'

Then he set off. He walked up Shore Road, waving again at Mr Crellin – *mainstyr*, he must remember that – over old Laxey Bridge and up Glen Road. Passing the Woollen Mill he could hear the rhythmic clackety-clack as Mr Wood demonstrated weaving to a youth group of some kind. Their mini bus was in the car park and Mike saw Mrs Bodmin who helped out in the Presence of Mann gift shop housed in the mill buildings, appear from behind it. He waved, but she hurried over to him so he had to stop:

'Hello, Mike. You're going today then?' Inwardly Mike groaned. How many more people had his Mum told.

'Yes, Mrs Bodmin.'

'It's a long way, indeed it is. Have you got sandwiches?' Mike brightened slightly:

'Not many Mrs Bodmin. Dad said I'd only eat them on the way.' Much he knew, thought Mike disgustedly.

'Wait there, lad.' She bustled away. Above the gift shop was the excellent CraftTea Weaver tea room with delicious cakes. At least Mike had been told they were delicious; he'd never had the chance to try any himself. He shifted from side to side; his PE teacher said that you mustn't get stiff if you were going to do a lot of exercise.

'Here you are, Mike. That will put you on a bit.'

'Wow. Thank you Mrs Bodmin.' Mike prodded the package with an exploratory finger and it felt gooey and rather heavy. He stowed it with his sandwiches.

'Best wait 'til you're out of Laxey, or your Dad might see you. *Traa dy liooar* you know.'

St George's Woollen Mill

'Yes, Mrs Bodmin, thanks again. *Traa dy liooar.*'

He plodded on past Cooil Roy. He wished he had a proper rucksack and not a carrier bag like a wuss, but maybe Dad would get him one of those as well, when he got to the top. Crossing what used to be the washing floor for the mines he passed Lady Evelyn, the Snaefell water wheel which had been brought back from Cornwall. His Mum said that visitors often mistook it for the Lady Isabella, as the larger waterwheel was more difficult to see from the road. He climbed up to where the Laxey Mines Railway was working, ferrying people up the valley, and watched one of the tiny steam trains squeeze through the miniscule tunnel. His Dad had paid for him to ride on it once, and he now knew exactly how toothpaste felt when squeezed out of a tube.

One of the volunteers, in dirty red overalls on top of an equally tatty sweater, saw him looking over the wall and came over:

Locomotive Bee, *driver, guard, coach and passengers, Laxey Mines Railway*

'You're Michael Trent aren't you?' and, when Mike nodded, 'it's today is it?' Mike looked up into a soot blackened face and didn't recognise it.

'Er… yeah?' The man laughed:

'It's Bob Mylchreest. You can't see me under all this dirt!' Mike tried not to gape at him. Mr Mylchreest lived next door and worked in a bank. In a suit. And a *tie*.

'Oh. Um. Sorry Mr Mylchreest.'

'That's OK. It's after eleven; you haven't got very far yet, have you?'

'No. I had to go down to the sea, and I saw Mr Crellin and Lisa and then Mrs Bodmin.'

'And now me. Well I won't detain you. You've still plenty of time. *Traa …*'

'*…dy liooar,*' finished Mike. Mr Mylchreest laughed and wandered away to oil something technical.

Mike climbed the rest of the way to the road, crossed it and turned to wave to the MER car which was whistling across the road behind him. The conductor waved back. Mike didn't know his name, but he'd seen him about. Surely he couldn't be another one who knew about the trek up Snaefell?

Past Ham and Egg Terrace, past Dumbell's Row and past the Heritage shop – he could see another of his Mum's friends through the window and hurried on in case he was stopped again.

Sites and Stories

*Two great ladies.
Left, Lady Evelyn;
below, Lady Isabella*

Then across the footbridge behind the fire station. He'd rejoin the road higher up.

Emerging from the trees Mike saw the Lady Isabella above him. People who hadn't been there agreed offhandedly that, yes, it was big, it was very big, but Mike remembered a visitor from England talking to his Dad, after he'd visited it for the first time: 'It's… it's so BIG. I mean it's really, really BIG.' Arms spread the visitor couldn't find words to describe something so enormous. Mike grinned at the memory:

'What are you laughing about, young Michael?' He reluctantly turned:

'Nothing Mrs Brightman.'

'Don't you cheek me, young man. What are you doing so far from home? Nothing good, I'm sure.'

'I'm walking up Snaefell, Mrs Brightman.' He tried for innocence and it almost came off. Silly old biddy, he thought. He wasn't doing anything wrong, so why pick on him.

'Oh, it's today is it?' (Not another one!) 'Which way are you going?'

'Up through Agneash and along the old miner's road.'

'To the Sneafell mine. Yes, I see. Be careful at the top. Crossing the stream can be tricky. It's best to stay as high as you can. If I remember rightly there's a footpath sign at the end of the miner's path. Best to follow it.'

'You've been up there?' Mike was startled. She almost smiled.

'Yes, I've walked up there. I wasn't always this old you know.'

'*Traa dy liooar*', muttered Mike. She looked at him sharply

'*Traa dy liooar*, indeed young man.

THE GREAT LAXEY WHEEL Built 1854 Designer Robert Casement

20½P ISLE OF MAN

1983

J. H. Nicholson RI

Questa

Now, if you're going on, go. Don't hang around or you'll never get there. It's almost lunchtime as it is.'

He turned back to the road and laboured onwards. Talk of lunch made him instantly hungry and he thought of investigating Mrs Bodmin's package, but he knew that while it was wrapped up he wouldn't eat it. Unwrapped however…

The road climbed steeply now and hairpinned to scramble up the shoulder of the hill. Few cars came this way and Mike walked in the middle of the road – which he was not allowed to do – swinging his bag – which was also forbidden. He tried to whistle but it came out as a sputter; he must ask Dad how it was done. He'd just reached the old pump by the wall at Agneash when he heard a groan. Mike stopped and looked round uncertainly. He seemed to be alone. Then the noise came again. Definitely a groan. Then a thwack from the gate of a house nearby. Rather nervously Mike went to investigate.

On the other side of the gate lay an elderly lady. She was waving her stick energetically and had managed to hit the gate with it, obviously to attract his attention. She could move and she could speak. What she couldn't do was get up. She looked up and Mike looked down:

'Well, young man. Are you going to rob me or help me?'

'Help you of course!' Mike was offended. Then he saw that she was doing what his Mum called 'being brave'. He opened the gate, walked in and knelt down beside her, saying rather diffidently:

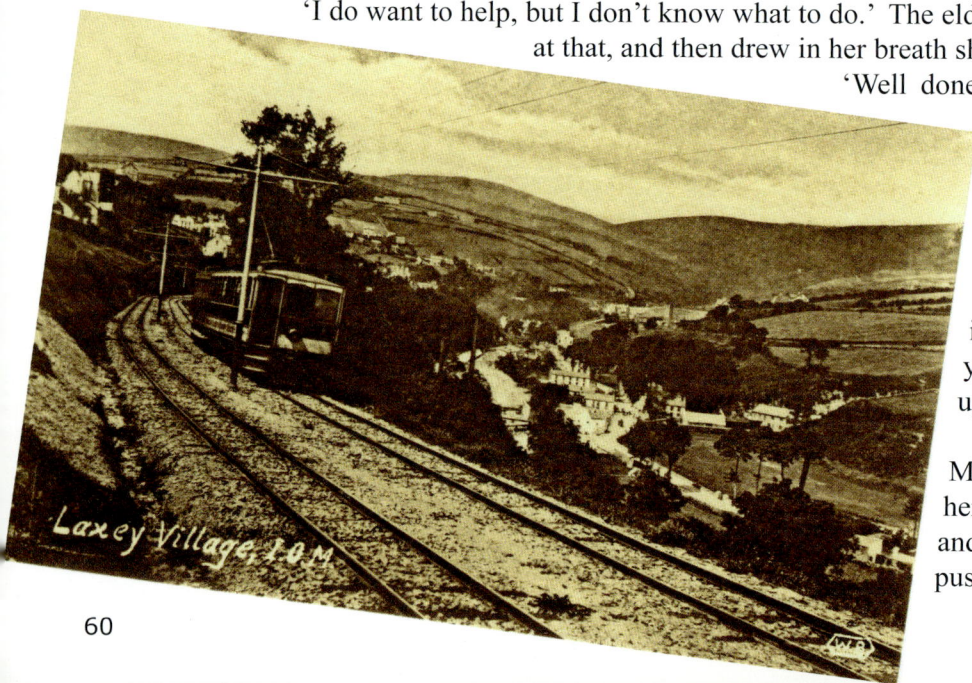

Laxey Village, I.O.M.

'I do want to help, but I don't know what to do.' The elderly lady laughed at that, and then drew in her breath sharply:

'Well done, young man. I do like it when people ask rather than treat me as though wrinkles on the face mean gaps in the mind. Can you help me to sit up?'

Rather gingerly Mike braced her with an arm and pulled as she pushed. He felt

60

Agneash. What looks like a path on the opposite hillside is the track of the Snaefell Mountain Railway

something grind rather horribly inside her and heard her mew with pain:

'I don't think this is good for you, Mrs…um?' She'd gone white and had lain down again.

'Smith. Yes, I know, I know. I've had problems all my life with Smith, but that was the surname of Mr Smith when I married him, and a good honest name it is. So was he. Gone now, poor love.' She chattered on bravely but her voice was weaker.

Mike felt in his pocket for his phone. He wished he'd remembered to charge it up, but it might work. He felt both excited and shy about ringing 9-9-9. It seemed so melodramatic somehow. But it had to be done:

'I'm going to ring for help.' Old eyes met young ones. She was frightened.

The call went better than he expected. He couldn't give the emergency services much information about who she was and, when he said Smith, they suspected a hoax – the old lady had been right about that – but then he had the idea of holding the phone to her head for her to talk to them. That got their attention. They promised to send an ambulance straight away. Mike was to do nothing except keep her warm and talk to her.

Inevitably he told her about his walk from sea to summit. His mentioned his ambition to own boots, and his hope for a rucksack as well. She asked about his limp and, for once, he didn't mind, as she obviously walked with a stick too. He said, without his usual defensiveness:

'I got polio. I caught it from someone who'd been to a country where it was. They were going to give us injections at school but I got it first and they had to make sure I didn't give it to anyone else, so I didn't go to school for ages. I didn't get it too badly but I had to learn how to walk again. And I'm all behind at school.' Saying it wasn't so bad when it was to someone who was worse off than he was. 'And Dad's very keen on rugby…' his voice trailed off as it always did when he thought about Dad. And sport. And being able to do things.

'You've got to live your own life, young man,' the old voice was pained but brisk, 'don't try to do too much too soon or you'll set the healing back.'

'I know. *Traa dy liooar*.' Mike spoke drearily.

'People been saying that a lot?' He nodded.

'"Time enough",' she mused, 'I think there's a better translation.' Mike looked up in surprise. 'Oh yes,' she added, 'lots of people don't know that "*dy liooar*" came into English as "galore", so *traa dy liooar* is "time galore". Lots of time. I prefer that.'

They both became aware of a blue flashing light labouring up the hill, presumably with an ambulance underneath it, and soon a couple of paramedics bustled through the gate. Mike was relegated to the sidelines as they worked. He spoke up firmly though when they were carefully loading Mrs Smith into the ambulance:

'I'm coming too.' The paramedic wasn't unfriendly but was unsure:

'Are you a relation?' Mrs Smith called from inside the van:

'I'd like him to come.' It was enough. Mike scrambled inside.

The journey was actually a bit boring. He'd hoped for sirens and squealing tyres, but no such luck. He couldn't see out of the window and the inside of the van was of no interest to him as he'd seen most of the equipment before. He couldn't even talk to Mrs Smith as she was wearing an oxygen mask. It looked a bit scary, but she winked at him, which made him grin.

When they got to Noble's hospital they whisked her away and left him in the waiting room. As it was now well into the afternoon he thought he was entitled to eat his lunch. The cake was a bit squashed but just as delicious as he'd heard. He also rang home.

His parents probably broke every speed limit between Laxey and the hospital, despite Mike telling them that he was only there because he was looking after someone else. As they hurried into the waiting room, a doctor pushed open a swing door:

'Mr Trent?'

'Yes, that's me,' said Mike's Dad.

'Mr Michael Trent?' Mike's Dad looked nonplussed. His name was Donald.

'Er… that's me,' said Mike.

'You're the young man who helped Mrs Smith when she fell?' Mike nodded. 'Well she's asleep now – we had to sedate her – but she made me promise to thank you. She said you were very kind and sensible.' Mike shuffled, mumbling:

'She'll get better?'

'Oh yes. She cracked a hip, but it isn't broken so she should be OK. In time. She said, if you asked about her, that I was to tell you "*traa dy liooar*".' The doctor uttered the phrase as though he'd never heard it before, nodded and excused himself. Mike's parents had been hovering. They came and gave him a hug:

'You did really well, Mike. You'd have got the whole way if it hadn't been for rescuing Mrs Smith,' his Mum was sympathetic. So was his Dad, who patted his shoulder (at least he's stopped ruffling my hair, thought Mike) and said:

'Next time, Son.' Mike knew they were disappointed, but oddly enough he wasn't. He was strangely pleased. Not about Mrs Smith's accident of course, but about helping. Being *able* to help. Something much bigger than the walk had happened. He'd proved he didn't need coddling any more. He could do his own thing now. He could even come back tomorrow to visit Mrs Smith. On the bus. On his *own*. He grinned up at two surprised faces:

'Yeah. No worries. *Traa dy liooar*, you know.'

FISHING, MINING AND THE GATEWAY TO SNAEFELL

Laxey would probably still be only a small fishing village, had it not been for the discovery of rich deposits of lead and zinc in the surrounding hills. Mining became part of Laxey life around 1780, but it was in the early 1820s that the industry grew to be the main source of income for local families, as well as attracting many who moved to the area chasing jobs. The scale and importance of the Laxey mines was such that their output of zinc per annum occasionally surpassed the total of all other British zinc mines put together.

For more than a century, life at Laxey revolved around the mines. The organisation of the various mining concerns was very complex, with several different mines operating in the area at different times, sometimes under the same management and sometimes independently. At the top of the Laxey valley was the Snaefell Mine, with Glen Roy mine over the hill to the south in Glen Roy and the North Laxey Mine a similar distance to the north in the Corrony Valley. The East Laxey Mine was also in the Corrony Valley and Dumbell's Mine around Agneash. The biggest of them all, the Great Laxey Mine, was at the base of the Laxey valley, with workings which stretched for several miles underground.

The remains of all this industry are still highly visible and an impressive reminder of the huge labour involved, in construction as well as excavation. Walk around Agneash, for example, and you'll see buildings which are the remains of Dumbell's Mine, whose shaft sank nearly a third of a mile into the ground. Stroll up Glen Roy and, even though the mine was unsuccessful, its wheel case still stands as a memorial to the miners who worked there. Ride up the valley on the Snaefell Mountain Railway and, on the opposite hillside and you'll see

Many of the buildings in Laxey, although now converted to other uses, would not have existed had it not been for the mines. For over fifty years the Mines Tavern, for example, was the house where the Mine Captain lived, although interestingly enough the mine never owned it. Part of the building was demolished when the electric railway was laid, which is why the trams pass so close to it. The public toilets near the fire station are housed in what was a compound for storing gunpowder. Dumbell's Row, although not originally built solely to house miners, certainly had a large proportion of mining families as tenants. Nicknamed Ham and Egg Terrace, many of the occupants ran eating houses from their front room and provided meals for anyone who could pay for them. Even the harbour would not exist were it not for the mines. The village certainly had a fishing fleet, but launched the boats from the beach. The harbour was built so that ore could be shipped out more easily. Even then, some tasks were beyond the capacity of the harbour equipment. Some of the castings for the Lady Isabella, for example, were too heavy to be unloaded from a ship by conventional means. They were brought into Laxey harbour at high tide, lowered over the side of the ship into the sea and then retrieved from the beach after the tide had gone out.

One of the few things in Laxey which seems definitely to be separate from the mining industry, is St George's Woollen Mill, more usually referred to simply as the Laxey Woollen Mill. Even this, in a topsy-turvy way, owes its existence to the mines, however. So many people were turning to the mines for their living and abandoning traditional crafts such as spinning and weaving, that experienced hand loom weaver Egbert Rydings became concerned. In 1871, John Ruskin, Victorian philanthropist and philosopher, founded St George's Company to address just such concerns as the neglect of traditional crafts – in 1878 the organisation became the Guild of St George and still exists. In the early 1870s Rydings wrote to Ruskin asking for help to do something about the situation in Laxey. In response the Guild sent Rydings sufficient funds to help found St George's Woollen Mill, which is of course where it gets its noticeably un-Manx name. Rydings took over the premises of what had been Moughtin's Corn Mill and started teaching local people how to make good quality cloth. Still run by the family of Robert Wood, who rescued it from liquidation in the early 1950s, Laxey Woollen Mill is now the only remaining producer of traditionally woven cloth on the island. Visitors to the mill can still see John Wood, Robert's son, at work one of the looms.

LIGHTS! CAMERA!...

A-a-and… ACTION!'

For the seventh time Malachi Jones strode through the castle's fortified gateway and up the steps leading to the keep. Gary Cooper in *High Noon*, he'd thought at first. Then he'd modified that to Hugh Grant in *Notting Hill*. Now he was getting closer and closer to Rowan

Atkinson as Mr Bean. He'd long ago given up trying to put anything into the scene other than walking where he was told and trying not to trip over his sword.

'Cut! CUT! Look, Freddie, love, forget the romantic lead stuff. This is the seventeenth century, the Civil War and all that. Your boss has just gone upstairs to deliver a letter telling the bird defending the castle that her old man is dead. Everyone's jumpy and someone might attack you with an axe. Never mind the blow dry, try to look hard, hey?'

The film crew sighed and shuffled their feet. Some of them glanced up at the lowering sky. They were there to film a documentary for the History Channel about the Manx patriot – or rebel, depending on your point of view – Illiam Dhone. As was the way with documentaries nowadays, some of the history was to be illustrated by dramatic reconstructions (Mathew Baynton, *Horrible Histories*?). This was one of them, but the only drama being reconstructed at the moment was that of the casting director. One of the bit-part actors had succumbed to a dodgy the whole it was. Not that he had any more dialogue (back to Mr Bean!).

He thought about his movie heroes. Perhaps that was the problem. Perhaps, rather than pretending to be Clint Eastwood or Harrison Ford or the Daniels, Craig and Radcliffe, perhaps he should just be Fred Jones (Stewart Granger, *The Prisoner of Zenda*). He surprised himself by liking the idea.

They wrapped for the day and Sam approached him:

'I wondered whether you'd care to come out for a drink? A group of us are going to the Castle Arms.' Fred smiled.

'I'd like that, thanks. Let me just get the armour off.' She raised one eyebrow and gave him a look which offered help.

'Meet you in the bar!' He'd have to explain that he was in a relationship. He wondered whether Neil would like her (Heath Ledger, *Brokeback Mountain*).

UK ISLE of MAN

Manx National Heritage
Castle Rushen

The Agency Ltd.

Manx National Heritage   2004   BDT

MEDIAEVAL MAGNIFICENCE

Probably the best preserved medieval castle in Europe and possibly the world, Castle Rushen is still one of the largest buildings on the Isle of Man. Its origins date from the middle of the thirteenth century when Magnus, the youngest son of Olaf II of Norway, became the ruler of the island. Peel Castle already existed, but the mouth and estuary of the Silverburn was at the time probably the island's most important harbour. What is now called Castletown Bay was sheltered from the prevailing westerly winds and protected to seaward by the Langness peninsula. Magnus wanted a decent fortification from which to defend important shipping coming to his new domain.

A few people wonder what Castletown was called before the town had a castle to be named after. The simple answer is that, before the castle existed, there was no town and so nothing to name. The settlement was across the bay and called Ronaldsway. Once Magnus Olafson's castle was built, a town grew around it and was named after it. The town even had its own stone church, St Mary's, possibly built by masons who had worked on the castle. That building is as the Old Grammar School and is thought to be the oldest continually roofed building on the island. After serving the local people for four hundred years as a church, the old building was extended and

Not Castle Rushen! The Old Grammar School, formerly St Mary's church, Castletown, possibly built out of stone left over after building the castle

adapted, and continued to serve them for a further two hundred years as a school. The school closed in 1930, but most of its fittings remain *in situ* for visitors to see.

The original castle was little more than a motte with a wooden bailey on top of it, later replaced by one in stone. Not much of Magnus's castle remains today after Robert the Bruce besieged and largely destroyed it in 1313. Twenty-one years after Bruce's attack, the English King, Edward III, granted William Montecute, 1st Earl of Salisbury, the right to rule Mann. The new ruler spent little time on the island, but did arrange for Castle Rushen to be rebuilt and expanded. Incidentally, about the name: in Irish and Scottish Gaelic (although not in Manx) *ros* means a peninsula, possibly with trees on it. There have been suggestions that 'Rushen' his letter contained the words 'the late Earl of Derby', as this was the first Charlotte knew of her husband's death. Grief stricken, she at first refused but, learning that the castle garrison was reluctant to fight, ceded victory on condition that she, together with her children, friends and servants, were free to go. The Manx retained their laws, and Illiam Dhone retained his importance to the English parliamentarians, becoming, between 1656 and 1658, also the island's governor.

The fall of Castle Rushen on 3 November 1651 gave Charlotte Stanley, Dowager Countess of Derby, the distinction of being the last person to surrender to parliamentary forces during the English Civil War.

For the next two hundred years the mediaeval fortress fulfilled several roles, including law courts, occasional meeting place for the House of Keys, a mint, one of the residences of the island's ruler, and the island's most secure gaol. In 1834, the Isle of Man's governor, Colonel John Ready, moved out of Castle Rushen and into Lorne House on the other side of the Silverburn, but the castle continued in use as a prison until April 1891. Another island governor, Lord Raglan, took it upon himself to restore the ancient building to its medieval glory and, in 1929 the castle was handed over to the Manx government.

The film industry on the Isle of Man is growing fast, and parts of the island have doubled for various places including South West Ireland (*Waking Ned*), Cornwall in England (*Stormbreaker*), a fictional Scottish island (*The Decoy Bride*) and Yorkshire in England (*Lassie*). Castle Rushen has featured in at least one television series, *Island at War*, where Castletown doubled for the fictional island of St Gregory in the Channel Islands. Castle Rushen also provided many of the interior shots for the film *I Capture the Castle*. However, no documentary about the Manx patriot Illiam Dhone has been filmed there. Yet.

OUR FEET MAY LEAVE BUT NOT OUR HEARTS*

And this is where we keep the bees.'

The visitors crowded round, fascinated by the view of the inside of the hive. One or two hung back and the guide reassured them:

'Don't worry. The hive is sealed behind glass so that the bees can't get out into the room, but you can still see what's going on.'

Fascinated, one little girl traced the path of a bee with a finger. The guide smiled at her and said, 'it's going to tell its friends where the best pollen is.' Sally ignored her.

Jan sighed. She'd always had problems with young children:

'Like most Victorian farmsteads, The Grove kept bees,' she continued to the mostly adult audience. 'Beekeeping was thought to be a suitable and elegant pursuit for Victorian ladies, and swarms were considered lucky. When The Grove was offered to the Manx people as a museum, the bees and the rest of the livestock were kept on. Of course, that's in the tradition of beekeeping – you can buy your beekeeping equipment but you must never buy the swarm. The bees will be offended if you do and won't stay with you.' Her small audience smiled tolerantly and one woman at the back asked:

'Why are they kept upstairs? Was it always like that?' The guide shook her head:

'Manx National Heritage installed the swarm up here so that the bees could easily be seen, but also so that they wouldn't alarm visitors. Bees aren't aggressive, but large numbers can

*From *Homesick in Heaven* by Oliver Wendell Holmes

be a bit intimidating. If they're flying out of an upstairs bedroom window, then they're well above visitors walking about at ground level. It's a good idea, don't you think?'

Beth Robinson smiled polite thanks and turned to look at the exhibits of farm implements, while other visitors crowded round. The guide, wearing a badge identifying her as 'Jan', stood back watching them. Visitors fascinated her; the odd things which interested them, their clothes – and that they seemed to know so little. Jan looked young in her Victorian costume, possibly no more than twenty or so. Over her tight, white bodice and long, dark straight-ish skirt she wore a pinafore, just as the two Miss Gibbs had done in their girlhood. Only her identification badge struck an incongruous note. She loved the house and enjoyed showing people round it, but didn't get the chance to do so very often.

She thought about the sorts of questions she was asked. Most frequently it was about the livestock: the loaghtan sheep, the pony-driven corn mill, the varieties of hens which Janet Douglas Gibb – 'Auntie' – had cared for, and, of course the bees, why they were here and why they were upstairs. She thought it an excellent arrangement. Imagine being able to supervise the hive, check the bees and collect the honey without needing to go outside. Long skirts soaked up mud and water from the clinging plants, there were none of today's waterproof and easy-to-wash fabrics, and changes of clothes were far less plentiful than nowadays.

She kept a close eye on the child. Children could be a problem, but at least this one was well behaved. Beth beckoned to her daughter and Sally trotted obediently over. Jan stepped quickly out of the way, but watched as mother and daughter inspected the Second World War uniforms – the label stated that they had been worn by Janet and Alice Gibb. She wondered whether the woman would look at the photographs included with the exhibit. If she did, would she notice the likeness? Jan loved it when people did. They'd look at her, look at the photograph and then look back at her trying not to let her see. Often she made it easier for them by pretending to be busy about something. If asked – which was surprisingly seldom – she admitted to the connexion. Occasionally, and usually only when the visitors had been more than usually demanding, she disappeared, leaving them wondering.

'Excuse me.' Jan turned and smiled a welcome. The couple who'd been listening to her earlier talk about bees had come back with another question.

'Why did neither of the Misses Gibb marry?' Jan's smile grew broader:

'Janet Douglas, the girls' Auntie, was the matriarch of the family and in charge of The Grove after the girls' grandmother died – their own mother ran a boarding house at Port Erin but couldn't afford to keep them with her. "Auntie" made the two girls promise not to marry. Her big fear was that the girls would leave and that the house she'd loved and lived in all her life would be left with no-one to look after it.' The woman looked incredulous and Jan laughed slightly:

'It wasn't just because of that of course. There were not many men available of the right class, and the girls were probably not a good enough "catch" – acceptable, indeed attractive, for a brief flirtation but being poor not a good proposition in the long term.' The visitor nodded but was reluctant to accept the fact and Jan was emboldened to go on. 'It's my belief, though, that the real reason they never married was because they never saw anyone they liked well enough.' This time the agreement was enthusiastic.

The idea of choice rather than duty was much more in keeping with today's considerations, yet Jan wondered. The two sisters had enjoyed life, she knew. Would they have been happier marrying and leaving the home they'd known all their lives. Or had they had the best of it, not tied to the whims of husbands and children. She didn't know; would never know now.

The departing guests clattered downstairs. Beth sketched a farewell. Her daughter looked merely bewildered. The wooden treads of the stairs had always made a terrible racket, and, if Jan had had her way, she'd have had them carpeted now. But it wouldn't be authentic of course. Descending slowly after the visitors she thought about that promise to Auntie.

The Robinsons walked back down the driveway to the entrance. The little girl was tired and starting to be whiney, but a promise to buy her an ice lolly at the gift shop staved off too much complaining. As she and her father considered the brightly coloured options available, Beth Robinson chatted to the staff:

The Grove

'It's so nice that some of the guides are in period costume.'

'You're… what did you say?'

'It's nice that some of the guides are in costume. Dressed in keeping with the house…'

'But none of our guides are wearing period clothing. We've often thought it would be a nice idea but have never got round to it. No funds.' The woman smiled, expecting understanding. Beth didn't return the smile:

'But the guide stationed in the room upstairs… the one in the room where the bees are…' Beth stopped as the two women glanced at each other. One said with what seemed unnecessary firmness:

'No member of staff is stationed in the bee room. There's no need.' Beth smiled vaguely as she paid for her daughter's lolly. It wasn't worth arguing about – and often the staff in these places weren't properly briefed. She wandered back out into the sunshine to admire the loaghtan sheep her daughter was trying to coax near enough to pat. Sally had forgotten about her Mum talking to someone who wasn't there.

Behind her the two women eyed each other:

'That's the third this week.'

'Should we mention it?'

'Well, they didn't believe us last time…'

Back at the house, Jan watched the caretaker lock up and leave. Alone she wandered through the house which continued to be her home. It was Alice's turn tomorrow. Fading from sight Janet Gibb reflected that she and her sister were still keeping their promise to Auntie.

TAKING YOU BACK IN TIME

A Victorian time capsule, The Grove was occupied until the 1970s by the last members of the family which built the house. The family's preferences and finances meant that their home had changed very little since the middle of the nineteenth century when it was extended from a single storey Manx croft to the small Victorian middle class dwelling it is today.

In 1838 Liverpool merchant and shipowner Duncan Gibb purchased 'the dwelling house outbuildings lands and premises situate in the Parish of Lezayre in the Quarterland of Ballavarcheen, commonly known as "Poplar Grove".' Gibb was returning from visiting the Point of Ayre lighthouse, then only twenty years old, and happened to pass Poplar Grove, which was for sale. Going in, he bought it on the spot.

Poplar Grove's fresh greenness must have been a real contrast with the dirt, noise and overcrowding which was Liverpool in the summer. Not only was the town a major port for all transatlantic trade, it was also a principal point of departure for emigrants from Britain and continental Europe. It was feared that migrants carried disease – some did – and their temporary accommodation in the town was less than clean. In addition Liverpool, in common with many major cities, was home to several violent gangs, thievery was on the increase and sectarian violence more common. Gibb wanted to get his wife and children out of Liverpool, for at least the busy summer months, and saw his new purchase as a holiday home.

Of course, being a wealthy – at this point a *very* wealthy – merchant, Gibb didn't consider his impulse-buy suitable for his family until it had been extended in almost all directions. The original Manx cottage makes up what is now the kitchen with its range and low ceiling. Above

that was added an upper storey providing rooms for staff and children. A large extension was built to the south, with greater headroom containing the family and formal rooms comprising entrance hall, drawing room, dining room, two principal bedrooms and dressing room. The different heights of the original vernacular building and the grander extension, explains the different levels of the landing upstairs!

The Grove – the Poplar part of the name was dropped quite early – might have become the holiday home of a middle class family, but that didn't mean that it didn't continue to be a small working farm. Duncan Gibb was a largely self-made man and wouldn't have allowed one of his acquisitions to languish for want of investment. Nor would he have neglected making what income he could from his purchase. The Grove lands at that time amounted to twelve acres and Gibb either bought or rented at least twice as many more. The resulting farmland was mixed dairy, sheep and arable – as it still is, although no longer part of The Grove – and so had work for a small farm threshing mill.

Windmills certainly existed on the Isle of Man. The best example is possibly the so-called 'witches mill' near Castletown, now residential accommodation. The Ramsey equivalent, Lezayre Mill, was only about a quarter of a mile south of The Grove; its truncated tower is now part of Beaconsfield Towers residential care home. Even so, mills on the island were more often driven by water, as the wind could be too strong for safe mill working. Duncan Gibb, however, wanted neither wind- nor watermill. He had been born in Greenock in Scotland and the farm mills he saw as a boy were driven by horsepower. He installed a pony-driven threshing mill at The Grove which, according to the house records, he purchased from Scotland. The Horse Mill at Wester Kittochside Farm in East Kilbride, not too far from Greenock, is almost exactly the same as the one at The Grove. Threshing separates the grain (the edible part of a cereal crop) from chaff (the husks and stalks) and is the first stage in the production of flour. Many farms did their own threshing and then took their grain to a commercial mill to be ground. Before the advent of the horse gin, The Grove's farm workers would almost certainly have taken the threshed grain to Lezayre Mill. After the horse gin was installed they may have done all the grinding on site.

Horse gins not only powered small threshing machines, but also provided the energy to run other small machines which would previously have been worked by hand – rather like mains or battery electricity runs small pieces of equipment today. In most places horsepower gave way to steam and it became much more economical for grain once again to be sent away to be turned into flour. The land occupied by the small farm mill was converted to other uses. Not so at The Grove. Like much of the interior of the house, the horse mill is a rare survival.

For many years The Grove remained a holiday home. The family visited regularly during the summer and a small permanent staff looked after the buildings and land all year round. That changed in 1862 when Duncan Gibb, now aged seventy, sold his business and retired to the Isle of Man. His family at that time consisted of his fifty-three year old wife, his widowed sister and his two unmarried daughters, Janet Douglas and Mary, aged twenty eight and twenty six respectively. Of Gibb's other five children, the two elder girls were married and living in Scotland, two boys died as babies and his surviving son was working for the East India Company in India. It was this son, also called Duncan, who was driven from India by poor health, married a Manxwoman and lived for a time on the Calf of Man before eventually settling in Port Erin.

Duncan Gibb the elder only enjoyed his retirement for five years, dying at The Grove in November 1867. His Will was a problem. It looked eminently fair, dividing all his property equally between his wife, his children and their heirs. Unfortunately that meant that The Grove no longer belonged to a single owner. The usual wording is to leave the spouse a life interest in the property in which she is living. That Gibb didn't do so meant that Mrs Gibb could have been turned out of her home by her children. The family was far too close knit to do anything of the sort, particularly as at least three of the owners – Mrs Gibb and her two unmarried daughters – were still living in the house. The joint ownership did however mean that any substantial change to The Grove needed to be agreed, in writing, by all the owners. As some

were on Mann, others in Scotland, and Duncan junior, at least for a time, in India or Canada, reaching agreement would have been time consuming to say the least. The logistical difficulty surrounding any change is one reason why The Grove has remained relatively unaltered. The other main reason was lack of money.

Duncan Gibb senior had been very wealthy, but, towards the end of his life, a combination of bad luck, sharp practice by rivals, and the occasional poor decision of his own, diminished his fortune considerably. After his death the family first tided themselves over by selling land and, when that had gone, resorted to stringent economy. Fortunately they still had enough land to make what might now be

called a smallholding, so vegetable gardens, orchards and a few cows and hens supplied much of the food for their table. Janet Douglas Gibb ('Auntie', see below) was particularly successful with egg and chicken production and kept several different breeds of hen. In addition, as was almost traditional for Victorian countrywomen – the President of the British Beekeepers Association from 1878 to 1906 was a woman, Lady Angela Burdett-Coutts – the Gibb ladies kept bees.

Bees have always held a special place in country lore as they are the only insect which makes a food eaten by man. In addition honey was one of the few sources of sweetness available before the widespread use of commercially produced sugar; it was also used in home-made remedies. The Grove became particularly noted for its honey, and bees are still kept on site in a specially constructed hive with a glass wall to allow visitors to see bee society at work.

Despite increasingly straitened means, in 1886, when Duncan Gibb junior died leaving a young wife and three children, Mrs Gibb offered a home to her son's small daughters after his death. She realised that her daughter-in-law would be hard put to earn enough running a gentile boarding house in Port Erin to support herself and her baby son, never mind educating and providing for her girls.

The Grove was a matriarchal house almost from the start, inhabited as a holiday home by the women for longer periods than the men. When it became the family's permanent home and after Duncan Gibb senior had died, its occupants were his wife, two daughters and widowed sister. Two years after his sister died in 1884, The Grove became home to Gibb senior's two granddaughters Janet and Alice, his wife ('Granny'), and his daughters ('Auntie' and 'Aunt Mary'). Genteel poverty became the norm, where appearances had to be kept up no matter how straitened the income. The Gibb girls, Janet and Alice, had fashionable dresses and were always turned out well, but there was little food in the larder and few people saw them toiling away by lamplight making their costumes from their Scottish cousin's cast offs. They often commented that it was a good job the Scottish cousin was stout as both the Misses Gibb could be kitted out from one of her dresses.

Janet and Alice Gibb moved to The Grove in 1886 when Janet was eight and her sister two years younger. Although regularly visiting their mother and brother at the other end of the island, the two girls lived at The Grove for the rest of their lives. Having outlived their immediate family, Alice died in 1971 and her elder sister in 1974. Before they died they ensured that their family home would be preserved for future visitors to enjoy it. This of course was the third reason, just as important as multi ownership and lack of funds, why The Grove survived unchanged. It was the Misses Gibb's home, filled with family memories and treasures, and they liked it that way.

Sites and Stories

FIFTY-FOUR DEGREES NORTH, FIVE DEGREES WEST

M ind the telescope!'
'I… I'm sorry. It's just it's so dark.'

'Of course it's dark, you idiot. It's night-time, it's supposed to be dark.' Paul was annoyed. Didn't the stupid girl know how much telescopes cost? He remembered her ratty jumper – knitted by her granny for goodness sake! – and thought condescendingly that she probably didn't. She should be pleased to be invited up here. The top of the Milner Tower was perfect, he considered. And not only for star gazing either. Pity she wasn't a looker.

Blaanid fell silent and wondered what to do next. With his film-star looks and his parents' wealth Paul was a natural magnet for the girls at school. Trouble was he knew it. After he'd had got his telescope – a gift from uninterested parents – most of the girls in Blaanid's class had immediately become stargazers of the astral rather than filmic sort. Not that Blaanid really blamed him. She'd probably have been similarly self-centred if boys had been throwing themselves at her. Which they hadn't. Tall and with a good figure she lacked the face to go with it.

'You going to help then?' Paul wasn't gracious.

'Uh, yeah, sure.' She obeyed his various instructions to hold this and do that, while he bolted the telescope onto its tripod and focussed it at the sky. At school he'd discussed his new pastime with carefully understated nonchalance. Blaanid suspected that he only valued the telescope as providing a reason for him to be out at night. What was merely another craze for him, was driving crazy all Blaanid's friends. Trysts had of course been arranged to 'look at the stars', and a number of different girls had come to school whispering triumphant innuendos. Having worked his way through the A list, it was Blaanid's turn. She knew that most of her friends would give their Cath Kidston bag (if they had one) to be in her place.

Looking up at the heavens she was overwhelmed, as always, by the sheer grandeur of it all. South west she saw Aquila. Almost due south was Capricorn. East was Taurus with its orange-red 'bull's eye' star Aldebaran. If she looked inland she could see Perseus with, below and to the left, Auriga. Higher up in the sky was Draco. That constellation always made her think of Harry Potter, and she wondered fleetingly where J.K. Rowling got the names of her characters from.

'I think we can just about make out Ursa Major and the Pole Star', Paul said.

'Can we really? Gosh.' Blaanid hoped she wasn't overdoing the naïve enthusiasm. Just make out the North Star indeed!

'Yes, it's a good night for it. Sometimes it goes into occultation.' Paul spoke off-handedly as though he'd turned down the job of presenting *The Sky at Night* in order to finish his A levels. Blaanid sighed. He did look gorgeous.

'Occultation? What's that?' At least he got the explanation mostly right she thought. It was indeed when something in the sky, usually the moon, obscured one of the stars behind it. It would never happen with the Pole Star though. Idiot. Blaanid was from an old sea-faring family. For years her relatives had navigat-ed with little more than the stars and the currents to guide them and she'd become fascinated by the tiny lights of distant worlds. She'd grown up know-ing the help – and the hindrance – of starlit nights. She'd also grown up know-ing to keep such knowledge dark.

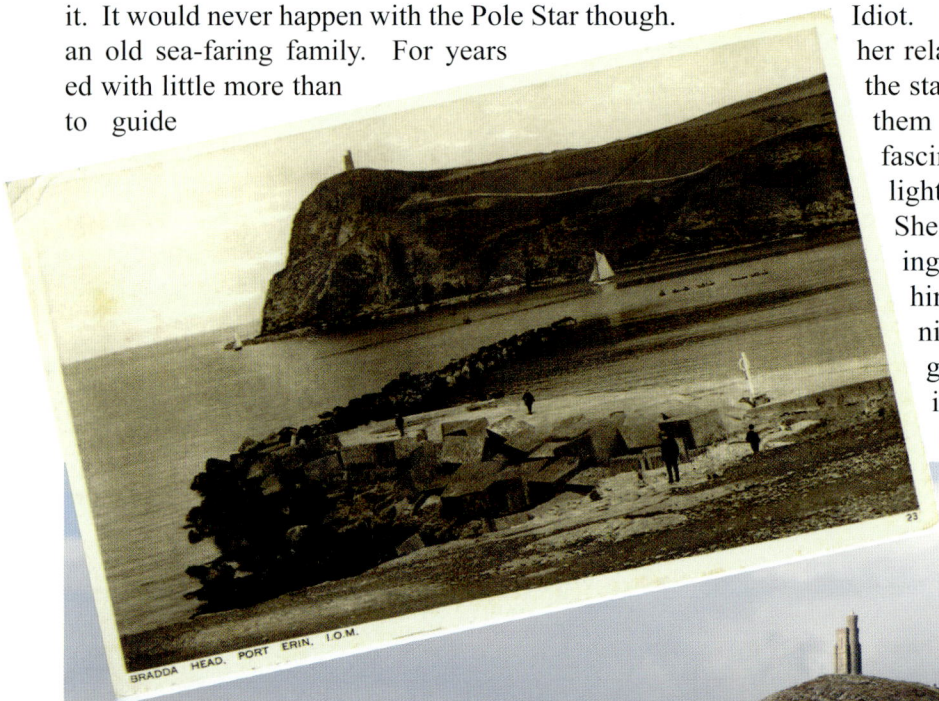

BRADDA HEAD, PORT ERIN, I.O.M.

As she gazed upwards she felt an arm circle her shoulders. She tried not to tense up. The setting was impossibly romantic and Paul intended to take full advantage of it:

'Oh, look!' she squealed, pointing, 'is that a UFO?' Really, she thought, could anybody be quite so daffy as that. Paul frowned and glanced up without interest:

'Probably the International Space Station,' he said loftily, and wondered whether anybody could be quite so daffy as that. Still she was here so… Blaanid broke away from him and clasped her hands together:

'Oo! I didn't know you could see the space station from here!' Trying not to sound too absurd and fearing she was failing she unslung her binoculars. Committed astronomers knew that you could get almost as good magnification of the stars using a good pair of binoculars as using the sort of telescope most amateurs would buy. And field glasses were both more portable and easier to use. She wouldn't forget lugging all that equipment up the very narrow, very steep and a very tight spiral staircase. Although the ISS could be seen, and seen clearly, on Mann, Blaanid had a feeling that it was over somewhere west of North America at the moment. Still, she hadn't seen anything anyway, so it didn't really matter. Her elder brother worked in the Isle of Man space industry so tended to know things like the orbits of satellites, distances between celestial bodies and the current position of the International Space Station. For once she was grateful for his chatty geekyness.

Paul was frustrated. He didn't usually have this trouble with girls. Grumpily he said 'I doubt whether you'd be able to see much through those.' Then he realised that, with her arms up to her face she couldn't see what he was doing. Moving round behind her he reached round to fondle her breasts.

Blaanid hadn't expected that. She jumped, dug her elbow into his chest and stamped back onto his foot. Uncle Juan was a sailor on board a Norwegian cargo ship and had been inveigled into teaching his nephews and nieces some basic self-defence. Paul recoiled, tripped over the tripod of the telescope and windmilled backwards to crash very satisfactorily onto the floor. He lay supine seeing a different sort of stars. She crouched against the wall waiting for his reaction.

'Damn. Oh damn, damn,' he moaned. To her relief he was making too much noise to be hurt in more than his pride. Eventually he rolled over to survey the damage. 'Look at this. Ow!' He sucked the base of his thumb, now bleeding from being jabbed with something which shouldn't have been sharp. 'Something' had broken, although it was impossible to guess at what.

Raging at her Paul scooped up the damaged 'scope and headed down the stairs. His impressive exit was rather spoilt by him having to turn sideways to edge down the stairs. It

was completely ruined as he had to make three journeys to move his kit. As he came and went Blaanid crouched in the corner of the platform. She wasn't going to help him. After returning the second time Paul looked resentfully at her shaking shoulders:

'You OK?' He obviously was itching to get away.

'Mm.' She sniffed and foraged in her back pack for a hanky. Boys hated girls crying. They didn't know what to do. Neither did Paul. He backed off hurriedly, tripping a little over the uneven pavement. Then he turned and squeezed down the stairs for the last time.

Moving very quietly Blaanid leaned over the parapet and craned to peer down at the doorway at the bottom of the tower. She could just about see. Paul stomped down the hill, his arms full of equipment. She had no idea how he would get all his stuff back without her help, but didn't care. Stifling the laugh she'd been holding on to for the last ten minutes she straightened up. The hanky had been a good idea. She hoped he'd gone soon enough.

A pity about the telescope she thought. She didn't like damaging something like that, even if it had been showy rather than much good. Paul grabbing her had been useful if unpleasant; her reaction put a stop to things very effectively and also ensured that he wouldn't want to repeat the experience. Most importantly he wouldn't suspect. OK, the girls at school would think she was mad, but she hadn't accepted Paul's invitation up here just so that he could grope her. It really wouldn't have done for him to have been using his telescope here tonight. He might have looked out to sea. And he might have seen more than stars. It would be high tide in about an hour's time and her Uncle Murcard was carrying on the family business. He was due in about now, heading for one of the little coves they'd always used. The family wouldn't touch drugs. Dirty money her *jishag* always said. And, since cousin Jamys had died from lung cancer, tobacco was a definite no no. There was always a good market for cheap booze though, no questions asked. Some of their customers went back generations. And Paul's Dad worked in the customs house…

DEMANDING DARKNESS

The Milner Tower perched 400 ft above the sea on Bradda Head is one of those rare manmade landmarks which harmonises with its surroundings rather than imposing something alien onto them. The effect is probably partly because it was built out of local stone. Erected in 1871, it is, unlikely as it seems, a monument to a Liverpool safe-maker.

Several stories are told about William Milner including one that he moved to Port Erin after a public demonstration of the strength of one of his safes went badly wrong and a young

boy was killed. According to the tale, Milner was so full of remorse that he retired from active business and devoted himself to charitable works. He certainly provided much needed financial help to the town's poor, and particularly struggling fishermen. One of his schemes was to build a breakwater to shelter Port Erin harbour. Either when the first stone was laid, or after the breakwater was completed – stories differ – Milner organised a huge party for everyone in the area.

He must have been highly popular as the tower memorial was built during his lifetime. It was supposed to have been paid for entirely by public subscription but, when the money ran out, Milner was so flattered that he paid the rest of the cost himself. The tower is square with a circular turret containing around forty steps attached to the east wall. The whole is said to be designed to resemble one of the Milner keys standing on end.

Before the mid eighteenth century there was no smuggling on the Isle of Man. Not because Manx seafarers were more or less honest than sailors of other nations, but because there was no need. Up until 1765, Tynwald set the rates of Manx import duty, independent of any interference from neighbouring islands, and Tynwald had decided that there would be little or no import duty on any commodity which could be resold. Consequently smuggling simply didn't exist on Mann; if everything can be imported legally and without financial penalty, there is no need to trouble to hide what you're doing. Taking it from Mann and importing it into England or Scotland was another matter however. What was honest trade on Mann, was subject to taxation across the water, and the Manx understandably took trouble to avoid paying unnecessary sums to foreign exchequers. Like their cousins the Cornish, the Manx considered avoiding the revenue men to be almost a national pastime. Also like the Cornish it was a sport they became very good at.

1707 saw the Act of Union which united England and Scotland. It was also a century which involved much of Britain in costly foreign wars. The British government was desperately short of funds (nothing new there) and so decided to increase taxation to raise more money (also not new). One of the easiest taxes to levy was on goods purchased. Naturally people resented the extra cost and just as naturally tried to avoid paying it. Smuggling grew from a few fishermen bringing home the odd luxury into a large-scale, well organised and highly profitable business.

From its position in the middle of the Irish Sea, the Isle of Man was ideally placed to take advantage of the high import duties imposed by the government in Westminster. Large trading vessels could and did land with impunity in the various Manx ports and along the island's coast. Having paid the much-lower duties on the island (or not) it was an easy matter to reorganise cargo into smaller vessels and slip across the sea to waiting customers in England and Scotland. Almost every Manx family had some seafaring connexion and virtually all seafarers were involved with some sort of trade, legal and otherwise. In fact so many Manxmen were selling luxury items across the water that they created almost a glut in trade.

It was the smuggling activities of the Manx, and more particularly their success, which led to the end of the island's independence. Pressure was put on the Lord of Man, John Murray 3rd Duke of Atholl, and he was forced to bow to what was effectively a compulsory purchase order. In 1765 the British parliament passed the Isle of Man Purchase Act, known as the Act of Revestment, which reabsorbed the lordship of Mann into the English crown and ended Tynwald's control of Manx taxation for two hundred years.

Immediately, acts of parliament – that's the Westminster parliament, not Tynwald – were passed to check smuggling, and, two years later, to levy new customs duties. Of course, the Revestment Act, having made smuggling illegal on the Isle of Man, actually encouraged its growth. Even families not actively involved in the trade connived at any opportunity to resist the laws of their new rulers. Uniquely, one of the vessels purpose-built for Manx smuggling survives, discovered walled up in the cellar of a family home. *Peggy* was built for George Quayle in 1789 by W.S. Yarwood Ltd. of Northwich, and possibly named after Quayle's mother. Originally designed for fast rowing and sailing she was later adapted to be purely a sailing boat and also appears to have been armed with small cannon. She was fitted with a sliding keel, often called a drop keel – a new invention at the time – which, when down, prevents sideways movement but which, when retracted, makes the boat easy to bring close to shore. It also has the advantage of enabling small boats to carry more sail and so make them faster. Officially a mixed cargo and passenger boat, there's little doubt that *Peggy*'s primary role was as a smuggling vessel.

Murcard is a Manx name which means sea expert (*jishag*, incidentally, is the Manx for 'Dad') and Manx mariners were highly respected. Many crewed the ships of discovery which sailed to the new world and the antipodes with only the stars by which to navigate. In many cases modern astronomy still uses the names given to constellations by the ancient Sumerians and Greeks. Capricorn, Perseus, Aquila and Draco, for example, were all first recorded by Ptolemy. More obscure is why the ancients thought that particular star patterns resembled things like a goat (Capricorn), eagle (Aquila) and charioteer (Auriga) when, to modern eyes, the description looks nothing at all like the object it is describing. Every culture has names for the stars which pattern the sky. The plough, for example, is an asterism – that's a small pattern of stars within a larger constellation – in the constellation of Ursa Major. The asterism might be known as the plough in Britain but is the big dipper in both North America and Russia (*Большой Ковш* – '*Bolshoy Kovsh*'), the salmon weir (*Otava*) in Finland and the medicine man's cart (*Göncö lszekér*) in Hungary. The French call it the saucepan (*le Casserole*). Each people names it after some object whose shape it resembles and to which they give some importance. The Vikings also knew the seven-star pattern and called it either the great waggon, as many countries still do, or possibly as Odin's wain (*vagn Òđin*). It is possible that the Manx, with their Viking heritage, might have done the same.

Unfortunately most of the current Manx names for stars now appear to be merely translations from the Latin used by foreign rulers. The plough, for example, is *Yn Cheeaght* (the plough), Capricorn *Yn Goayr* (the goat) and Aquila *Yn Urley* (the eagle). The same thing happens with Auriga which is translated as *Yn Fainagh* (the chariot). This is interesting as *Fainagh* comes from *fainey* which means 'a ring', so the Manx word for chariot is actually a description of something with rings (wheels). The Manx people's own names for their stars appear in many cases to have been lost, but we do know that the Milky Way is known to the Manx as *Raad Mooar Ree Goree*, or the Great Way of King Orry.

Many places on the Isle of Man have no artificial lighting, so are ideal for observing the night sky. Seven sites around the island have been designated 'Dark Sky Discovery Sites', the highest concentration of such sites within the British Isles, and more are planned. The island's lack of light pollution means that the sky is very visible from the island, but the island is not at all visible from the sky. NASA astronaut, Nicole Stott, photographed the Isle of Man from orbit when aboard the International Space Station in 2009 and commented:

'I tried on many occasions to identify the Isle of Man from orbit, but I had great difficulty because it is so dark! I eventually captured an image and it shows how wonderful the night skies in the island are. The Manx skies are fantastic for astronomy – great from both above, on board the International Space Station and from below, on the Island'.

The Isle of Man is becoming increasingly involved in aerospace technology and is fifth after China, the US, Russia and India in the race to return to the Moon. The highest capacity satellite in the world, ViaSat-1, was placed in space by an Isle of Man team and is now providing broadband access to rural areas of the United States. Excalibur Almaz, based just outside Douglas, offers commercial space transportation to anyone who wants it, and is planning space tourism in the near future. The Isle of Man aerospace team was

also involved with the Phoenix Mars Lander. With a Dutch company seriously floating the idea of colonising Mars in the foreseeable future, the Manx specialists might be called in to help. Now that really would be a giant leap for Mann-kind.

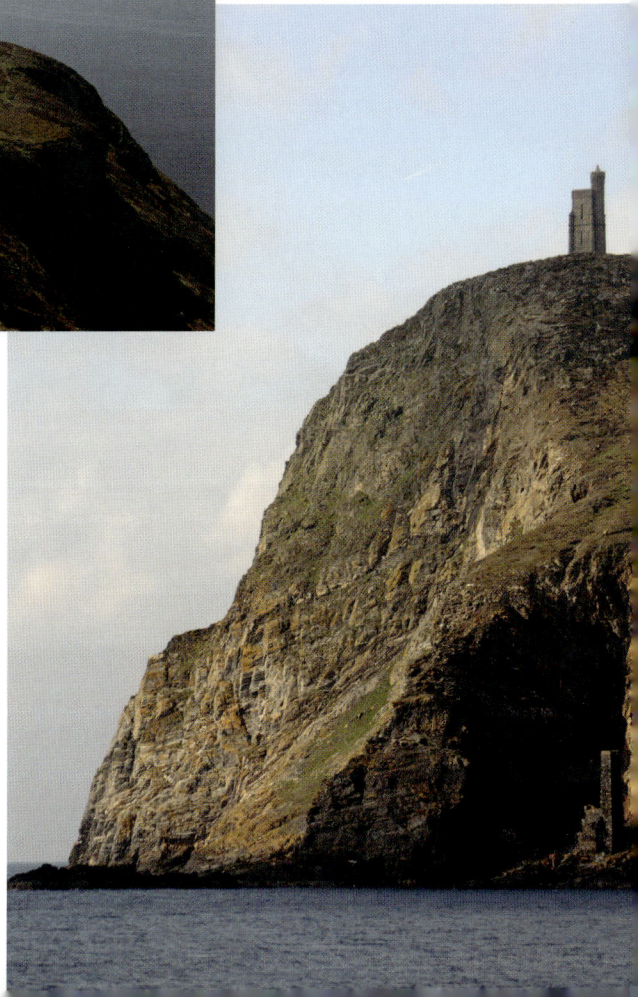

ONE DOG AND HER MAN

The UK visitors were impressed. Delegates from the Rare Breed Survival Trust, various farm parks and living museums, and the University of Reading had all asked intelligent questions about period crops, soil and yield. Animal specialists had queried husbandry. Demonstrations of thatching, spinning, woodworking and making Manx quilts had all been duly admired. Problems of visitor access had been aired, shared and solutions discussed. Administrators had sympathised with each other about tea rooms, loos and paperwork. Even Orry the Manx cat had been patted and petted. Best of all the weather had been stunning.

Gorgeous blue skies, a slight breeze, the scent of the gorse and the sparkling of the sea. Cregneash was showing off its best.

Now came the final event of the conference. A sheep-dog trial between Beamish Living Museum, Cotswold Farm Park and Cregneash, with the Rare Breed team acting as judges. It was all very friendly of course, but there was definite rivalry.

Sheep herding using dogs was not officially demonstrated at any of the three establishments taking part, but in each there were keen individuals who practised privately. Bob Hawkins with Spot from Beamish had just missed third place at the Northern Open, John Robinson with Bess from Cotswold had been Highly Commended at Lydthorpe, while Martin Kelly with Dhoo used to be a regular feature at the Royal Manx Agricultural Show. He'd been missing for the last couple of years and there was much speculation that Dhoo had been ill. But, there she was, bright-eyed, body quivering with eagerness.

Neither the ground nor the time had allowed for anything more than a basic course and it was smaller and shorter than was usual. Cregneash had provided fifteen loaghtan sheep for the event and one of the great imponderables was how they would react. The prehistoric breeds were not used to being herded by dogs and were not usually used for sheep-dog trials. As well as entertainment and friendly competition the trial was also designed to test whether herding

demonstrations using loaghtan sheep would be a possible draw for the public:

'It's not authentic,' grumbled one agricultural historian. His colleague was more pragmatic:

'Neither is selling ice-cream. If this sort of show attracts more paying visitors then it's all to the good. We can use the money to research what is authentic.' Overhearing, Martin Kelly was sardonically amused. Husbandry turned into a sideshow to raise cash. What was farming coming to? His old Dad would… he didn't finish the thought. His old Dad wouldn't have approved of his actions today.

He and Dhoo had drawn the final run, so he took the dog to the sidelines to give her a drink. He'd already assessed the course, crouching to get a dog's eye view – funny how some people didn't do that – and had realised that the breeze which made the hot day pleasant for people, didn't stir the grass at ground level. It was baking down there. The dogs in their fur coats would suffer if they had to work for long.

He looked at the dog. She was a beauty. Unusually for a Border Collie she had no white on her. Hence her name of course. Dhoo meant dark or black in Manx. What was startling was her eyes. They were bright blue. Blue eyes weren't uncommon in Border Collies, but with her dark fur they shone like two points of light.

The organisers called for the first entrant and Bob stepped forward with Spot at his heels. The five loaghtan were released from the holding pen, the clock started, and so did Spot. The outrun was faultless, with the dog arriving directly behind the sheep. The lift wasn't so good. Border Collies herd by using their eyes, eyeballing the sheep until they give ground and move away in a bunch. Spot was having trouble. He was too strong. The sheep were moving, but it was more of a panicked scatter than the bunched trot the dog – and man – was aiming for. By

MANX LOAGHTYN RAM

P 20

ISLE OF MAN

J.H. NICHOLSON R.I   1973   COURVOISIER S.A.

Sites and Stories

dint of constant running backwards and forwards to slow the gallop and retrieve strays the dog got the sheep round the course but it was a scrappy performance. Bob was annoyed, Spot had shown badly and the shepherd's praise was grudging.

Martin frowned slightly. The dog had worked his heart out for his master and was badly overheated. It wasn't Spot's fault that the sheep weren't used to dogs.

Cotswold John had seen Spot's performance and was looking uneasily at the next lot of sheep. Bess at his side quivered with anticipation. She had the reputation of being very strong-eyed and was excellent with a large flock on the wide limestone hills of home. Whether she could be as good in the smaller, steeper Cregneash field, with the smaller, wilder Manx sheep John wasn't sure.

He was right to be anxious. The round was a disaster. Poor Bess did much more than was asked of her and that was the problem. She pushed too hard and sheep fled in all directions. One even scrambled over a gap in the wall. Watching intently Martin approved of the shepherd. John was very good with her. Flustered, the dog had got disheartened and her master concentrated on restoring her confidence rather than worrying too much about the course. He concentrated on getting her to bring each sheep to the pen where he could hold them safely. It took four fetches for five sheep but he was patient and praised her efforts. Those knowledgeable among the spectators approved. The points didn't matter; the dog did.

Then it was Martin's turn. Dhoo stepped lightly beside him, turning her face up to his. Five new loaghtan were released and the shepherd sent the dog away. To the spectators' surprise Martin whistled a couple of times during the outrun. Directional whistles were not permitted; the dog should know where to position herself. After the two previous rounds the scoring had largely been forgotten but he lost a lot of points for it.

Dhoo dropped lightly behind the sheep and started nudging them forward. Her blue eyes stared towards the small flock and they gradually drifted away from her towards Martin. If the outrun had been poor, the lift had been very good indeed. Martin wiped his sweating palms on his corduroys. The dog needed no instruction from him. The sheep trotted down the slope, the dog weaving behind them to keep them straight. They only baulked when they saw Martin. He lifted his fingers to his mouth and whistled softly, denying even to himself that he shared his Dad's old prejudice against shepherds who used a mouth whistle. Dhoo came closer, circling

Rose Cottage in May 2008 (above); now known as Quirk's Croft (left). Work continues; the lean-to (or is it a loom shed?) is now also thatched

and the sheep wheeled and headed off diagonally away from him just as they should. The dog passed close to her master, looking up at him.

'Good girl,' he muttered, 'take time.' Dhoo slowed and the loaghtan eased through the gap made by a couple of hurdles. They looked a bit agitated, but not too bad and were at least sticking together. Again Martin whistled and again the dog circled to bring the sheep to the cross drive. The loaghtan didn't like this. They wanted to go down the slope and the dog was in the way. The spectators all held their breath. Lose it now and all the good work was undone. The biggest of the loaghtan stamped and turned to face down the dog. The sheep's four horns made a large St Andrew's cross around its head. To the dog below, the shape of the horns was clearly outlined against the sky. Dhoo crouched, staring at it intently. The loaghtan hesitated. Shook its head. Glanced away. And… turned. Bustling together, the small flock completed the rest of the drive. Some of the spectators applauded.

Martin was tempted to forego the shedding. It would be difficult for Dhoo, and she'd done so well. But that would have meant giving the competition away. And to the chap who'd been hard on his dog. Martin assessed the loaghtan. Two of them were wearing red collars and the flock looked calm enough. Dhoo was holding them, waiting. The theory was easy; separate the two collared sheep from the other three. Martin strode into the shedding ring. Dog and man manoeuvred the small flock. It turned and turned again. Slowly, slowly the two marked sheep were brought together. Martin lost points again for doing more of the work than the dog, but it was still good work and everyone held their breath. Then came the command: 'in here'. Dhoo dived between the two groups and the two red-collared sheep galloped away. The dog chased after them to bring them back, and again Martin's whistles brought her to position. The experts watching began to have their suspicions about why.

The sheep had been excited and Dhoo had some trouble controlling them, but they'd got used to her by then and didn't put up too much resistance. Penning them was almost an anti-climax. As sometimes happened, the animals seemed suddenly to co-operate in their own capture. As Martin closed the gate his 'that'll do' was heartfelt. Dhoo ran up, tail wagging, eyes bright. As he bent to fuss her Martin thought it was such a shame there was so little light in them.

'The lass is going blind. Vet says there's nothing can be done.' Martin glanced down at Dhoo lying on his feet. The Port Erin pub was warm and the delegation full of good Manx beer.

'So that's why you've not been at the Royal Manx?' One of the show's organisers emptied his glass appreciatively. Martin nodded:

'My old Dad would have had her shot. "Can't be feeding animals which don't work" – all that sort of thing. But I couldn't do it.' Martin sighed. So did Dhoo. 'I've been working her in the fields and found that her nose mostly told her where the sheep were, providing I gave her a bit of help to get into position behind them. She knows the work, and can still see a bit, enough not to run into walls or over cliffs. Then when this competition came up I wondered whether a dog which wasn't so strong-eyed might be better for loaghtan. Spook them less…' He tailed off, not sure whether he was making sense and afraid of being sentimental.

'And you were right!' John, his hand on Bess's head, was generous with his praise. He grinned, 'showed the rest of us up!' Then he lifted his glass:

'To Dhoo!' 'Dhoo!!' they chorused.

Beneath the table Dhoo dozed, ears twitching. She was dreaming. Of grass under paws. And Martin. Trotting sheep. And Martin. Whistles. Martin.

That'll do.

CROFTING LIFE

In Manx terms Cregneash has always been considered one of the most isolated villages on the island. Even in 1889, *Brown's Popular Guide to the Isle of Man* could say: 'The village… consists of about a dozen houses, and was, until the last few years, noted for its persistent retention of the old ways and ideas of the country. The community, small as it is, rarely married outside its own limits. They kept up the old habits and dress of their fathers; Manx only was spoken among them; none of them had been out of the island except during their fishing voyages, and many of them had never been outside the limits of their own parish… Their houses were low, roughly built huts thatched with straw, while bundles of gorse placed in the doorways served instead of doors…'

As most visitors know, the open-air museum which is Cregneash began with Harry Kelly's cottage. Harry's forebears had lived in Cregneash for more than three centuries and he himself was the last native Manx speaker, i.e. the last person who spoke only Manx. Because his native tongue had not been diluted by knowledge of other languages Harry was instrumental in keeping Manx alive. Linguistic specialists from around the world visited him in order to learn about Manx in its purest form, and to record Harry speaking it.

It was one of these visitors, Carl Marstrander, Professor of Celtic Studies at the University of Oslo who, hearing that the Manx Museum was keen to create an open-air folk museum, suggested Cregneash as the best place to site it. After Harry's death, and hearing of the Manx Museum's interest in him and his cottage, Harry's nephew and heir donated Harry's old home and its contents to the museum. The cottage formed the nucleus of the first open air living museum in the British Isles when Cregneash opened in 1938.

Harry's Cottage is half lofted, which means that only half of the building has an upstairs. The loft is over the *cuillee* (back room or bedroom), while the *thie*

Cregneash

mooar (big house) was the combined living room and kitchen where the *chiollagh* (hearth or fireplace) provided warmth and cooking facilities. The *thie mooar* was open to the rafters, which were often made of wood recycled from something else. Until the last century there were relatively few trees on the Isle of Man, so wood was scarce and expensive. Many of the buildings in Cregneash have rafters made from recycled ship's timbers, including masts, spars and even oars. The sea would have provided a sporadic but welcome harvest of driftwood.

The spacious headroom in the *thie mooar* – the area where the loft isn't – was left so that threshing could be done inside the cottage. Threshing was a task for winter when long hours of darkness and poor weather meant that little could be done outside. Threshing parts the edible parts of a cereal crop, such as the grain, from the inedible (at least to humans) parts such as the chaff or protective covering. Threshing can be done by crushing the crop underfoot, putting it through some sort of machine or hitting it with a tool designed for the purpose. Called a flail, such a tool is often simply two sticks of wood joined together by something flexible such as a chain, hemp or leather hinge. One piece is grasped and swung, the other hits the crop scattered on the threshing board. It is hard work.

On large farms work such as threshing or winnowing would take place in a barn. Crofting, however, was farming on a very small scale and few crofters could afford the time, money or effort to erect a separate building for many of the farming activities. Those which required shelter would be done inside the house. A threshing floor of boards was laid over the puddled clay floor of the cottage,

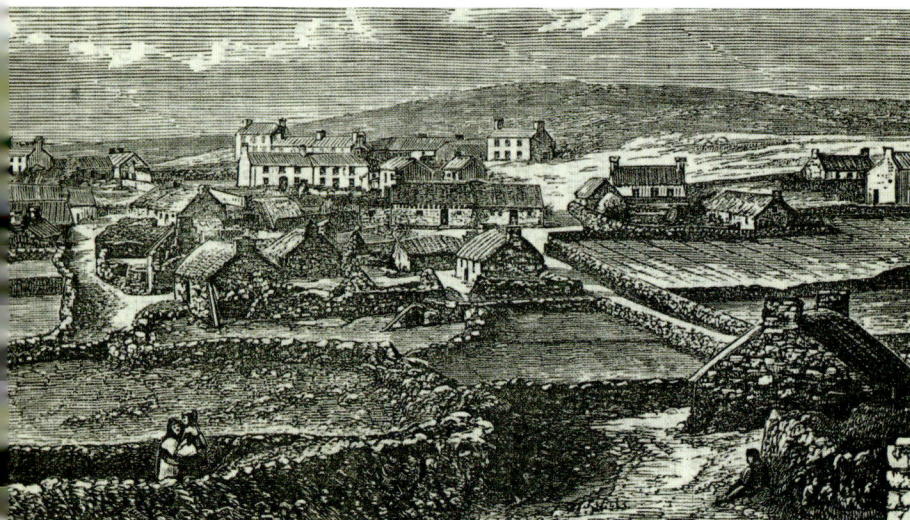

An engraving of Cregneash from Brown's Popular Guide to the Isle of Man, *published 1889, and the village today from the same spot. Although built in 1878, eleven years before* Brown's Guide *was published, the church does not appear in the engraving. Presumably Brown was reusing an earlier illustration*

and furniture such as the dresser and clock were covered with a sheet. The family would then take it in turns to flail their small crop and the coverings would protect the family's treasures from most of the flying dust. Incidentally, to prevent the precious grains escaping a board would often be used to block the lower part of the door, and it is from this board that we get the word 'threshold'.

Once the crop is threshed, the edible parts of the crop are still mixed in with the inedible, so the mixture is winnowed to separate the two. The cheapest way of doing this is to use a breeze, as throwing the mixture into the air allows the heavier kernels to fall to the floor while the lighter chaff is blown away. In Mann winnowing, like threshing, was often done inside the house to keep the crop dry. In Harry Kelly's cottage a blocked up door is visible opposite the entrance door. Many Manx houses were traditionally built with two doors opposite to each other in this way. By propping both of them open the cottager created a through draught which was enough to winnow the small crop.

When the only way to get anywhere was by walking, many of the skills necessary for life in a small upland village would have been available on site. The local joiner would not only have made or repaired agricultural tools, for example, he would also have made much of the furniture for the cottages. One of the most important of these was the dresser where items of use and decoration would have been proudly displayed. Because the joiner would make them to fit the space – and pocket – of the crofters, dressers can be found in all different sizes. Skilled joiners would also have been expected to make or at least repair the local women's spinning wheels. Every woman would have been able to spin, as the clothing and blankets for the family would have had to be manufactured from their own sheep. Once spun, the wool would have

Cregneash

been knitted or turned into cloth either on a home loom – four of the cottages at Cregneash still have *thie coigee* (loom sheds) – or by the local weaver.

The Manx loaghtan is one of the oldest breeds of sheep and, together with breeds such as the soay which are native to other islands, is the nearest modern equivalent of prehistoric sheep. The name, which is sometimes spelt loaghtyn or loghtan, is believed to come from the Manx words *lugh* (mouse) and *dhone* (brown) and probably refers to the attractive colour of the fleece and the animals' size. Lambs are dark brown and get lighter as they get older and as they are exposed to sunlight. Loaghtan are probably one of the few animals whose coat fades noticeably in the sun!

Under the auspices of Manx Heritage Cregneash still does much of its farm work by hand or using horse-drawn implements. The village blacksmith would probably have doubled as the farrier and would have been a very important figure. Not only would he have kept the working horses shod, but would also have co-operated with the joiner to make and repair agricultural and domestic equipment. No-one now knows where the original Cregneash smithy was as it closed before the end of the nineteenth century. However, early in 1960 a smithy of the appropriate size and type was however reconstructed in two sheds donated by Mrs Walter Karran and using building techniques copied from an upland smithy in Ballacomish, Arbory. Original and authentic tools were donated from other smithies around the island, which were closed or closing. In particular, Mr Kewley, blacksmith of Andreas, was retiring after well over thirty years, and donated most of the gear and equipment. The smithy might be new but it continues a tradition of blacksmiths going back hundreds of years.

Cregneash is generally recognised as the first living museum in the British Isles and is still one of the most unusual, not least because many of the buildings in the village are still privately owned and inhabited. In the non-museum part of the village visitors are just as likely to see a be-suited businessman as a bonneted Manx cottager. Yesterday's farming community supplemented their income by fishing, while today's might raise extra cash by tourism. The means may be different but the end is the same. Not much has really changed after all.

OLD MAN

The old man shivered. Blimey it was cold up here. A rock didn't make the warmest seat and his bum bones were going numb. Nightwatchman was a young man's job – perhaps he should call it a day at his age. Still, he'd been doing this a long time and was used to watching for threats. Besides he wasn't about to let any of them Nazis attack his island. Some of them were even living here, but locked up, at Peel, just as they should be. Not that he was a bigot. Oh no. Some of his best friends were foreigners. He'd liked that lot who'd come over from Anglesey. Fellow Celts the Welsh. They'd treated him right. And not all

the Germans were bad. Some of them they'd got in the camps over at Onchan were just as frightened as his own people living outside the wire. He'd looked into Teutonic faces and seen the terrors of old persecutions. They were no threat, he knew, but he also knew that those in charge had to be careful.

Second World War they were calling this one. He scowled into the dark. You'd think one world war would have taught those in charge some sense, but, no, they had to go and do it all again. Some power-man in a posh office thought that another power-man in another posh office across the sea had done something which couldn't be sorted out by talking. Then all the young people trooped away and started to kill each other. Years ago the leaders put their own necks on the line, leading their troops into battle and often dying in the process. He had a sort of respect for that. Nowadays the power-men stayed safe and got other people to do their killing. And dying.

He'd never understood it. Wars! He could tell them about wars. He remembered the last one. And the one before that. Not that he'd left his island, of course. Protected occupation, that was what they'd called it, looking after the land, making sure people were safe and that there was food on the tables. Not much food and, come to think of it, not many tables, but people managed. They always had to manage when the power-men got it wrong.

He looked across to the old watch and ward points. Vikings had introduced watch and ward, he thought with satisfaction. Them old Norse seafarers knew a lot about fighting. Didn't do a lot else sometimes. Knew that an efficient early-warning system was essential in time of war. The Vikings, he thought with affection. Warriors and farmers. Looked after their land – like him.

He was amused that the same system was still working after all these years. Not as good as before of course, but nothing was. Rotas of men keeping a look out from high points around the Manx coast. Watching for attack from the sea. He wasn't part of any official watch – he hadn't bothered to volunteer, he knew they'd think he was past it – but he could still do his bit. Up here. Up on the roof of Mann. He'd still got good eyesight, despite his age, and could see it all.

He thought with scorn of the masts dotted about the countryside. Some new-fangled stunt they were, sprouting on various hills around the coast. Metal trees. First at Scarlett and Bride and now at Dalby. First it was to guide Manx ships, and then it was find other people's. Now it was the flying machines. Up at Douglas Head they'd even got a training school for it. The old hotel had been rechristened HMS Valkyrie, though why they want to pretend a building was a boat he couldn't think. RDF it had been called – radio direction finding – but now people were using the Yankee term, radar. Radar! He snorted. To his way of thinking, radar was just divining by another name.

He shifted slightly on his boulder and scanned the darkness again. He liked sitting up here. Nobody came up here at night. Nobody bothered him. In fact not many people even thought about him nowadays and he knew no-one listened to him. He didn't care. They'd realise one day, and he could still do his job, whether people knew about it or not.

The island spread itself beneath him like the folds of a robe, floating in the bowl of the Irish Sea. The rim of surrounding lands rode the waves, lightless, hiding themselves from view. By contrast the lid of the bowl was alight with stars. The old man ignored them. Offshore, a tiny glint had caught his eye.

A pinprick reflection of starlight in the midst of the ocean. Periscope? Perhaps. He'd heard it called that when he'd eavesdropped on some of them official watching posts. Hadn't known he was listening they hadn't! Some sort of seeing tube from beneath the waves, that's what a periscope was. Looking for ships. Well, no Manx blood was going to be shed on his watch. He'd always be ready for them.

Rising from his rock without haste, the old man stood sentinel on the summit of Snaefell. His form elongated like a shadow at dusk, reaching for the stars which swirled around his head like a diadem. Gathering himself, he seemed to grow younger as he grew in stature and authority. Taller than anything for tens of miles he became as he had always been, the final authority for the island beneath his feet. Almost casually he swept the ragged grey cloak from his shoulders and swirled it over the land. Mist spun from the tatters, lacing and thickening. Tendrils of grey cloud lengthened, grew, stretched and spread. Fleeces of fog knitted into a thick blanket, flowed between the hills and settled on the sea, cocooning the island he'd protected so long. Old Manannan nodded, satisfied. Let them find their way through that. Radar or not he doubted they could. This island was his. Would always be his. Visitors, welcome or not, would soon learn that Manannan protected his own.

HIGHPOINT ON MANN

For hundreds of years Man on Mann has watched the coastline, alert to any form of attack. With the threat of invasion very much in mind those living on the island organised a system of Watch and Ward lookouts placed around coast with the object of giving early warning. Instituted by the Scandinavian invaders, the system was manned and maintained for centuries and only started to fall into disuse after the defeat of Napoleon. Look-out points were designated for each parish and there is some information that different Watch and Ward posts were used by day and bay night. All men of the parish kept a

strict watch in turn. The only general exemptions to the rota were for the old, young and ill, although Members of the House of Keys and one or two other officials were also exempt by right of office. Snaefell itself was not part of the chain of look out posts partly because it was difficult to access and probably partly because it was often obscured by cloud.

Despite scientific advice suggesting that it should be included, Snaefell also did not form part of the chain of radar sites which protected Britain's coasts during the Second World War, and for possibly the same reasons. The mountain was considered too remote to man easily, and had to wait until 1956 for its planned incorporation into the radar chain. The white concrete building on the hillside above the point where the A18 road crosses the Snaefell Mountain Railway (SMR) was built in the early fifties to provide the operations block for

the new radar station. Before it could go fully operational however, the plans were shelved. Incidentally, although a single storey building, it is not this which gives the area the name of Bungalow. That derives from the single storey station building first erected at the crossing when the SMR opened in 1895.

The Victorians were very enthusiastic about new technology and particularly liked railways, seeing them as providing easy freedom of travel for the first time. It's rather startling to learn that all of the Isle of Man's railways were built in the twenty-three years from 1873 to 1896. The SMR was one of the last to be built and was always intended as a tourist railway. Five miles of track were carved into the slate of the mountain side in just seven and a half months during the worst winter in living memory. February was particularly bad, with the lowest temperatures ever recorded in Britain. Even low-lying Douglas had eight inches of snow while Snaefell – 'snow mountain' – lived up to its name with gale force winds, blizzards and snow drifts up to fifteen feet deep in places. Through it all the navvies battled on. The SMR was passed fit for use on 16 August 1895 and opened to passengers five days later. Today we'd probably not even complete the feasibility study in the time. The SMR had beaten the other British 'snow mountain' railway by a year; the Snowdon Mountain Railway opened in 1896. During its first year of operation, the SMR carried up to 900 passengers per day.

Possibly mindful of the weather, a small wooden building was erected at the summit as a waiting room for travellers, but soon became totally inadequate as the number of visitors grew. Building work soon started on larger and grander facilities and the Summit Hotel opened in 1902. It was a two-storey building, of stone and with mock gothic turrets and castellations. Although called a hotel, it did not offer residential accommodation, but was designed as a hostelry for travellers to purchase refreshments. After doing so for eighty years the Summit Hotel was gutted by fire in 1982. The blaze could be seen for miles and the fire brigade duly turned out, getting to the summit on the Victorian trams, but could do little other than contain the blaze once they got there, as there was no water supply on site.

The hotel's replacement is a much simpler single-storey building, although still performing the same function of providing refreshments. Even today there is still no piped water at the summit. The water in the cloakrooms comes straight off the mountain and is not drinkable. All provisions, including a bowser of drinking water, are transported daily to the summit on a tram which also carries the hotel staff. Visitors sitting enjoying a cup of tea and the view rarely realise that everything they are consuming has been carried on the Victorian railway.

Despite its inaccessibility, dinner at the top of Snaefell is not a new idea, however. On 1 July 1814, 1,500 people climbed up the mountain to celebrate the defeat of Napolean.

Thomas Dixon, landlord of the British Hotel in Douglas – the current British Hotel in Douglas harbour is a replacement building erected about fifty yards west of its namesake – arranged a cold collation for 120 of the climbers, in a marquee on the summit. Those enjoying the peak of dining included the island's Lieutenant Governor Cornelius Smelt, and General Goldie, who had fought under Wellington.

Inaccessibility was a feature of the Snaefell Mine too. Situated at the head of the valley, the miners path runs along the shoulder of the hill opposite the mountain railway. Miners living at Laxey had to walk the three miles to work, in all weathers, before starting their eight-hour shift. Never a particularly large or prosperous mine, the Snaefell Mine has the dubious distinction of being the site of the worst mining disaster on the Isle of Man and one which, understandably, traumatised the local community. A candle left burning caused a fire deep underground, which was not detected as it occurred on a Sunday, the only day when no work was done. Fire in in an enclosed space like a mine where there is a restricted amount of oxygen, produces carbon monoxide. The gas has no colour, taste or smell and is therefore very difficult to detect without specialist equipment. It is also very slightly lighter than air. When inhaled carbon monoxide prevents oxygen being carried by the bloodstream and can therefore also be deadly. On Monday 10 May 1897, not knowing of the contaminating gas, thirty five miners were lowered into the mine at the start of their usual shift. Twenty of them died. One hundred years later a plaque commemorating the event was placed on the capped shaft head.

Snaefell summit is only accessible by tram or on foot but the A18 provides ready access to much of the Manx upland. Perhaps surprisingly, the mountain road actually predates many of the roads on the island. Some of the mountain road dates from the deforesting of the early

The ruins of the Snaefell mine. The sealed head of the shaft is beyond the ruined building on the right

1860s when access was needed to remove trees from the lower slopes. Tracks which already existed were joined up, but much of the road was built from scratch, particularly the section from Keppell Gate, north west of Creg-ny-Baa, to near the Guthrie Memorial. The road was first incorporated into the TT race in 1911.

Being the highest point on the island, particularly as its peak is often covered by localised low cloud, Snaefell is a natural hazard for air traffic. Today night-flying aircraft are alerted to the proximity of the summit by lights on the masts of the radio station. During the Second World War the blackout made such precautions impossible. For planes stationed in Andreas or Jurby – both wartime aerodromes – and for those flying across the Irish Sea, the proximity of the mountain caused several fatal crashes. Experience was no protection. On 6 September 1953 Group Captain Worthington was flying Group Captain Richmond from RAF Millom, Cumbria to RAF Jurby, to replace him as commander there. His Avro Anson hit the south east shoulder of Snaefell about a hundred feet below the summit, killing all on board.

The cloud which frequently obscures Mann was traditionally thought to be courtesy of Manannan Mac y Leir the legendary ruler after whom the island is supposed to have been named. According to mediaeval texts Mannin McLir was a celebrated merchant and sea pilot who lived on the island and was skilled at reading the weather. Over the years Mannin became confused with Manannan, the Celtic equivalent of Neptune, and McLir transmogrified into Mac y Leir or son of the sea. Legend says that Manannan protected his kingdom by enveloping it in mist so that enemies couldn't find it and invade. Even today, low cloud is often referred to as the cloak of Manannan. The old sea god is still protecting his own.

SELECTED BIBLIOGRAPHY

Anon, *Industrial Archaeology of the Isle of Man; an introduction*, Manx National Heritage, 1993 amended 2006.

Anon, *Isle of Man 1993 Site Handbook*, 21st conference of Scottish Vernacular Buildings Working Group, 1993

Attwater, Donald, *The Penguin Dictionary of Saints*, Penguin, 1966

Bawden, T.A., Garrad, L.S., Qualtrough, J.K. and Scatchard, J.W., *Industrial Archaeology of the Isle of Man*, David & Charles, 1972

Bromet, Sir Geoffrey Rhodes, *Government Houses in the Isle of Man*, self-published paper, 1952

Brown, James, *Brown's Popular Guide to the Isle of Man*, James Brown & Son, 1889

Craine, David, *Tynwald; symbol of an Ancient Kingdom*, Printing Committee of Tynwald, 1976

Cubbon A.M., *Smithy Reconstruction at Cregneash*, article in *The Journal of the Manx Museum, Vol VI, No. 76*, edited by A.M. Cubbon and W.R. Serjeant, The Manx Museum, 1959-60.

Dubbeldam, Andree, *Wild Flowers of Mann*, Lily Books, 2004

Francis, Paul, *Isle of Man 20th Century Military Archaeology, Parts 1-4*, Manx Heritage Foundation, 2006

Freke, David, *The Peel Castle Dig*, The Friends of Peel Castle, 1995

Garrad, Larch S., *The Naturalist in the Isle of Man*, David & Charles, 1972

Goodwins, Sara, *A Brief History of the Isle of Man*, Loaghtan Books, 2011

Hellowell, John, *A Tour of Manx Lighthouses*, Peter Williams Associates, 1998

Kenyon, J. Stowell, *The Gibbs of the Grove*, second edition, Manx National Heritage, 1992

King, Sue, *A Weaver's Tale; the life and times of the Laxey Woollen Industry 1860-2010*, St George's Woollen Mills Ltd., 2010

Kniveton, Gordon (ed), *A Chronicle of the 20th Century Vols I and II*, The Manx Experience, 2000

Moore, A.W., *The Surnames and Place Names of the Isle of Man*, Elliot Stock, 1890

Paton, C.I., *Manx Calendar Customs*, The Folk Lore Society, 1939

Pearson, F.K., *The Douglas Head Suspension Bridge*, article in *The Journal of the Manx Museum, Vol VII, No. 85*, edited by A.M. Cubbon and Ann Harrison, The Manx Museum, 1969.

Pearson, Keith, *The Douglas Horse Tramway*, Adam Gordon, 1999

Poole, Steve, *Rough Landing or Fatal Flight*, Amulree Publications, 1999

Quilliam, Leslie, *A Gazetteer of the Isle of Man*, Cashtal Books, 2004

Quilliam, N.D., *Keys and Cuffs – the inside stories; the History of the Isle of Man/Manx Prisons 1417-2008*, N.D. Quilliam, 2009

Radcliffe, Constance, *Shining by the Sea*, Radcliffe, 1989

Randles, Jenny, *Supernatural Isle of Man*, Robert Hale, 2006

Rush, R.W., *Horse Trams of the British Isles*, The Oakwood Press, 2004

Scarffe, Andrew, *The Great Laxey Mine*, Manx Heritage Foundation, 2004

Scarffe, Andrew, *The Story of Laxey Flour*, The Manx Experience in conjunction with Laxey Glen Mills, 2010

Scarffe, Andrew (ed), *Laxey and Lonan Heritage Trust 25th anniversary edition newsletter 1987-2012*, Laxey and Lonan Heritage Trust, 2012

Stowell, Brian, *Abbyr Shen! Starting to Speak Manx*, Manx Radio, 1986

Wilson, David M., *The Vikings on the Isle of Man*, Aarhus University Press, 2008

Wood, James, *A New Atlas & Gazetteer of the Isle of Man 1867*, Mannin Collections Ltd., 2003

Woolley, Sue, *Peeps into the Past; a tribute to Syd Boulton 'An Editorial Legend'*, Suzanne Woolley, 2010

Yearsley, Ian, *When horses really pulled their weight*, article in *Tramway Review No 216, December 2008*, Historical Journal of the Light Rail Transit Association, edited by Richard Buckley, LRTA, 2008

ACKNOWLEDGEMENTS

I am indebted to several organisations and individuals who gave up their time to provide help, information and/or photographic material. They include, individuals: Joann Corkish, Suzanne Cubbon, Rhonda Cooper, Peter Kelly, Rachel Lapham, Jo Overty, William Short; and organisations: APA Architects, Hurstwic Viking Group, Office of the Clerk of Tynwald, Presence of Mann.

Always of course I am grateful for the support and photographic expertise of my husband, George Hobbs.

Thank you all for your help and assistance; any mistakes are entirely mine.

INDEX

Page numbers refer only to the most significant references within the text. Pages numbers in *italics* indicate illustrations; italicised pages may also contain relevant text.

Aerospace 90

Ballafayle stud 27
Beekeeping 75, *76*, 82
Blacksmith 98

Close Beg 53
Close Startfield nature reserve 54

Dark Sky Discovery 90
Double-decked trams *29*, 30
Douglas Head 35, 100

Fenella Beach 44
Film industry 74
Great Laxey Wheel
    see Lady Isabella

Harness 28, 30
Harry Kelly *95*
Harry Kelly's cottage 95-7
Home of Rest for Old Horses 27
Horse-powered mill 80-1

Iliam Dhone 67, 73
International Space Station 85, 90

Lady Evelyn *59*, 64-5
Lady Isabella *59*, *60*, 63, *64*, 66
Laxey mines 63-6
Laxey Mines Railway *58*, 65
Laxey Woollen Mill *57*, 66
Loading of horse trams 29-30
Loaghtan sheep 20-1, 91-4, 98

Manx Electric Railway 27, *60*, *65*, 66
Moddey Dhoo 46
Mountain Road 104-5

Old Grammar School, The *71*
Operation of camera obscura 36, 37

Orchid Line *54*

Port Skillion 36-37

Quarry Bends 55

Radar 100, 102-3
Round tower *42*, 43

Sanctuary stones *41*
Sagas
    see Storytelling
Slavery 21
Smuggling 88
Snaefell mine 63, 64-5, 104, *105*
Snaefell Mountain Railway *65*, *102*, 103-4
St George's Woollen Mill
    see Laxey Woollen Mill
St German's Cathedral *41*, 44-5, *46*
St John's Church 9, *10*
St Mary's Church
    see The Old Grammar School
St Patrick's Isle 43
Stars 84, 89
Storytelling 19, 22
Summit Hotel 103-4

Threshing 80, 96-7
Traditions 12, 46, 105
Training of tram horses 27, 28-9, 30
Tynwald Ceremony 6, 10-12

Viking buildings *14*, 20
Viking costume *15*, *17*, *21*
Viking ships *20*
Vikings 9, 11, 19, 100

Watch and Ward 100, 102
Wetland 52-3
Windmill 80